A Blow to the Head

A BLOW TO THE HEAD
a history of violence

Andries du Toit

Published in 2024 by Hands-On Books
Cape Town, South Africa
www.modjajibooks.co.za
Copyright © 2024 Andries du Toit

All rights reserved.

Andries du Toit has asserted his right to be identified as the author of this work. No part of this book may be reproduced or transmitted in any form or by any means, mechanical or electronic, including photocopying or recording, or be stored in any information storage or retrieval system without permission from the publisher.

ISBN: 978-1-991240-25-5
(ebook) 978-1-991240-26-2
Cover design by Masha du Toit
Design and layout Andy Thesen
All illustrations © Masha du Toit

For Maretha

We are fractal structures of our society. We do not heal in isolation; our healing is collective.
Sister Đẳng Nghiêm

Even though I looked close, I still couldn't see—
what was the trauma, and what was the tree?
Joshua M. Schrei

There is a path to take that has nothing to do with victory or defeat: a place we do not yet know the coordinates to; a question we do not yet know how to ask. The point of the departed arrow is not merely to pierce the bullseye and carry the trophy: the point of the arrow is to sing the wind and remake the world in the brevity of flight. There are things we must do, sayings we must say, thoughts we must think, that look nothing like the images of success that have so thoroughly possessed our visions of justice.
Báyò Akómoláfé

CONTENTS

Part 1	1
At the fitness club	3
"A regrettable incident"	10
A word about the times	15
Part 2	17
Cradock	19
The Koo Valley	21
Wivenhoe	28
Part 3	31
Critique in the world	33
The chisel	38
The comfort of enemies	43
Working	47
Part 4	51
Prominent people	53
Divisions	57
Part 5	65
Finding words	67
A shock	70
Keeping safe	75
"Naming and shaming"	77
Part 6	83
In the parking garage	85
Counting the cost	90
Healing nicely	93
Part 7	95
Aftermath	97
Feeling in the dark	100
Part 8	105
What is at stake	107
The kyōsaku	110
Turning around	112
Acknowledgements	115
Works cited	116

Part 1

At the fitness club

It's Friday morning, 5 February 2016. I am at the Kauai cafeteria at The Point Virgin Active health club in Green Point, Cape Town. This is not my usual haunt: usually I take my daily swim at the club in Wembley Square in Gardens, but once a week my routine brings me here. So today I am at the long oak table that stretches along the south wall, sipping my coffee, enjoying my post-swim smoothie, and catching up on the morning's emails before heading off to the office. All is well with my world.

And then this happens: a group of men join me at the table. I register them only peripherally at first—I have a dim impression of two sitting down opposite me, and at least one more man at another table. All in matching powder blue fleece tops. A team of some sort. They're in high spirits: jovial, ebullient, and making quite a stir as they put in their orders. Not minimal orders either. These men are large, and they have healthy appetites. I notice breakfast wraps, fruit salads, juices, smoothies and "flu shots" (shot glasses of fresh ginger or wheatgrass), the works.

At this stage of the proceedings I am inclined to view them kindly. They are big, burly, jovial, bluff and plainspoken. White guys. Afrikaans. The sort of dudes you'd find in a Deon Meyer novel, nursing a whiskey on the bar counter next to Bennie Griessel. "*Nee, dit gaan goed met my,*" one man is saying on the phone. "*Oorgewig soos gewoonlik, maar gesond*" (I am well, overweight as usual, but healthy). I look up and he is indeed a bit overweight, a big man with straggly facial hair, reclining regally in his chair. His companion is much fitter; a big man, also stocky, but it's all muscle and no fat, with close-cropped hair. He's leaning over his breakfast, shovelling it in with a will, saying "*Jis ja, as ek nou hier uitstap is ek fokken gesond!*" (When I leave here, I will be fuckin' healthy). With the part of my mind that is not focused on my emails I'm enjoying the pleasure this group of friends seems to be getting from their morning meal.

Gradually, however, I start to become uncomfortable. The black woman who is serving them—I will call her Vuyokazi, though that is not her real name—seems harassed and stressed out, and after a moment or two I get the impression that they are not being very nice to her. She was already taking strain when I arrived this morning, as the cafeteria's computerised ordering system is on the blink. Now she is running from pillar to post and apparently getting their orders wrong. She is familiar to me, and I know her to be a gentle, shy, rather diffident woman. Right now, she is not doing well. Part of the problem is that she does not appear to understand their Afrikaans. They are impatient with her and remonstrate with her unkindly and irritably. "Get it right this time," the big man is telling her. "I want olive oil." He pronounces it with an exaggerated parody of an African accent. "Aw-leave oil, OK?" She looks agitated. She scuttles off and returns with something, but she has not got it right. This time the man is clearly contemptuous. Again he asks for "Aw-leave oil" in a mocking parody of her way of speaking.

I don't like this at all. I don't like the discourteous way this man is talking to her, and I particularly don't like the way in which he is imitating her accent. I can see that she's rattled and believes that she's messing up in some way. And I think she can see that the man is mocking her, making fun of her as a stupid black woman.

At this point I am not sure what to do. I am irked by the man's crudeness, but also not sure whether I should intervene. He doesn't look as if he's being intentionally vicious. He's just being thoughtless and mean, getting a momentary kick out of making fun of a black woman. Will he even understand? I resolve to let it pass for now, but I also tell myself that if he continues, I will absolutely have to say something.

And sure enough, it happens again. The woman comes back with whatever she's bringing him, and he sneers at her again. "Aw-leeeve oil," he says. She looks on the verge of tears. That's it. I have to say something.

I think for a moment. I must be careful how I frame this. I can't just tell him he is being racist—he won't get it. He probably just thinks this is good, harmless fun. I wave at him to attract his attention and say to him, perhaps rather sternly: *"As mens so met iemand praat en hulle aksent namaak, dan kan dit die indruk skep dat jy met hulle spot. Dit kan as onbeleef of onbeskof voorkom. Dit kan ook as rassisties ervaar word"* (If you speak like that to someone, and imitate their accent, it can create the impression that you are mocking them. It can be seen as impolite or rude. It could even be seen as racist).

The man is visibly irritated and says something about the bad service in this joint. This is a global business, he says to me (in English). They need to do something about their terrible service.

He's not even getting what I am saying.

I repeat it again, more clearly. You have to be careful, these days. Behaving in this way, talking to someone mockingly like this can be construed as being discourteous, even racist.

He sits back and more or less ignores me. But his companion, the big lean one, looks over at me with narrowed eyes. He speaks in a low vicious undertone. *"Jou fokken poes, wie is jy? Noem jy hom 'n rassis? Jy het niks op ons te sê nie"* (You fucking cunt, who are you? Are you calling him a racist? You have no right to judge us).

I am a bit taken aback by this immoderate response. I dial down my asperity a bit. I explain that I was not saying his friend *was* a racist; I was pointing out that his *behaviour* could be *construed* as such. But he continues as if I have not spoken. He leans right across the table and tells me that he is giving me sixty seconds to get out of my seat and leave the club; if I am not gone by this time he will take me into the parking lot and fuck me up (*"Ek sal jou fokken opfok"*).

OK. Right. I seem to have gotten myself into an unpleasant situation. I don't particularly want to back down and run away—I am still in the middle of my breakfast and have an unsent email I want to finish—but it's also clear that this conversation is not going anywhere useful. And now he's actually starting to count backward. From sixty. This is ridiculous. I look over at the first man, who is now leaning back munching his breakfast and looking at his smartphone as if none of this concerns him. I think I might be able to defuse the situation by taking the conversation back to him. What do you think? I ask him, taking care to be as mild and reasonable as possible. Do you feel what I said was inappropriate? Did you take me to be calling you a racist? What's your view? He looks up from his phone with a look of mild warning. "*Jy beter na hom luister*" (You better listen to him) is all he says, as if his friend is a vicious dog that's best not provoked. Then he returns his attention to his phone.

His big friend continues with his abuse: "*Fokof uit my gevreet, of ek gaan jou fokken doodmoer*" (Fuck off out of my face, or I will fucking beat you to death). These threats are not shouted. They are delivered in a savage undertone with narrowed eyes, which somehow is much scarier. He looks as if he means it too. He continues with his countdown. I register how buff and muscled he is. I have no doubt that, though he may not literally kill me, he can certainly knock my teeth out. I suddenly recall a story from a few years ago about a young man who had his skull cracked by bouncers at a nightclub not far from here, in a dispute over a sound system. I don't know who this man is or what he does, but he looks like the kind of man who could do a thing like that. There is something chilling about his contained, feral rage.

So. What now? I'm at a loss. For a moment I consider calling management, but for some reason I discard the idea. Perhaps it is that I am still hoping to de-escalate the conflict. Perhaps in some corner of my mind I still think I can reason with them. Also, I have a strong sense that if I push back at them, if I get indignant with them in turn, if I cause a fuss, there's no knowing where it might end. I don't want to back down and be humiliated; but I also need to stay polite and calm.

Again I appeal to the first man. I say that I did not mean to offend them or cause a fight. Again he simply indicates to me that "*Jy beter na hom luister*" (You better listen to him). And then, rather unbelievably, the second man lurches out of his chair and walks around the table. He's finished his countdown. I register that he is huge. He seems to be walking with a limp. He comes right up to me and leans over me, continuing his torrent of abuse, calling me a *poes* and threatening to kill me. Then his face works oddly for a moment (I wonder, absurdly, whether is about to have a fit). And then he spits in my face.

It is a surreal moment. As they say in the classics, this seems to be happening to someone else.

I realise three things:
1. There's not much actual saliva involved. Perhaps his mouth is dry.
2. My attempts at de-escalation do not appear to be working.
3. If I continue sitting here, trying to reason with them, or ignoring them, things are just going to get worse. While I don't wish to interrupt my breakfast, perhaps I could consider simply moving to another table.

I get up (rather shakily, if truth be told) and start collecting my things. I am conscious of feeling embarrassed, and (somewhere) a little furious. I don't know how to handle this. My attention is mostly focused on trying to appear unruffled. The big man continues his abuse, with the first one joining in. They are now calling me a *kafferboetie* (kaffir lover). They are telling me that they will come round with their coloured friends and fuck me up. They tell me to go back to the black people I love so much. That I probably pay black whores to suck my cock. (This last in English). The first man also tells me that they are not going to leave the matter here. He says I'd better not go and complain to management or there will be trouble. He says that they will be able to follow me: "*Ons weet jy ry Toyota. Ons sal jou soek en ons sal jou kry*" (We know you drive a Toyota. We will look for you and we will find you).

Now I'm really unnerved. Up to this point all this has just been humiliating and unpleasant. But I do in fact own a Toyota. How do they know this? I have never seen them before today. If they really know who I am, and are threatening to exact violent revenge at some point in the future, I've got to take all this more seriously. These are not people I want to meet in a dark alley late at night.

For now I say nothing. I muster what little dignity I have left, pack my things and leave for another table.

The other people at the oak table, and the other tables around us, act as if nothing is happening.

I finish my coffee and continue with my emails. Or I try to. I am rattled. This is not over. The two men go on eating, laughing and joking, perhaps feeling heartened by their victory. They are joined by Powder Blue Man number three, who has been watching events from his table. At some point the manager of the cafeteria joins them in hearty discussion. They are laughing and joking. Should I make a fuss now? Should I call Virgin Active management? Again, for some obscure reason, I decide not to. I don't want to provoke a confrontation, with management mediating between me and two (possibly now even three) men who, going by trends thus far, are not going to take a reasonable attitude. I'd rather wait and work here until they go.

Then I become aware that the second man is trying to attract my attention. I get up but he comes limping over to me. He's still spewing abuse at me in a vicious undertone. "*Jy fokken kom as ek jou roep, jou fokken poes, jy ignoreer my nie*" (You fucking come if I call you, you fucking cunt, don't you dare ignore me). He notices my laptop. "*Kan jy fokken Google?*" he says. "*Google my naam. Jy sal sien ek is die grootste fokken criminal in Kaapstad. Ek gaan jou fokken doodmaak, jou poes*" (Can you Google? Google my name. You will see I am the biggest fucking criminal in Cape Town. I am going to fucking kill you, you cunt). I try to point out to him that I can't Google him if don't know his name, but he does not seem to pay attention. Then the first man comes over too. Again, I try to reason with them. "*Ek het nie bedoel om julle te beledig nie. Kan ons dit laat staan? Kan ons vrede maak?*" (I did not intend to insult you. Can we leave it? Can we make peace"?). But this has no effect. They simply continue with their verbal abuse and with threats that they will follow me and slit my throat ("*fokken keelafsny*").

Again they go back to their table, and I to mine. I decide it's time to call management. I catch the eye of the floor manager (he appears to have been watching) and he sits down at my table. A young black man, radiating friendliness and mild concern. I explain to him what has been happening. I explain that I don't need him to intervene right now, but that they should just keep an eye on things; when they are gone and the matter is sorted I will decide what to do. But while we are talking, the first man approaches me again. He takes out his smartphone and elaborately, very ostentatiously, takes a photograph of me. He obviously wants me to understand that they intend to use this to identify me in future. (Later I realise that the thought of *me* taking a picture of *him* did not even cross my mind). Eventually they leave, with the second man continuing with his threats ("*Ek kry jou in die parking lot*"). My heart is pounding. I stare at him impassively and don't respond.

"A regrettable incident"

ALL THIS HAPPENED MORE THAN eight years ago. I remember every detail. I wrote it all down, pretty much as I have recounted it here, later the same day.

Other memories are fragmentary. I recall driving to work just after this happened, feeling shaky, on the verge of tears. Helen Suzman Boulevard was bright and busy. The world was going about its business unchanged. What had just happened? Was I in danger? As it happened, no one had been lurking in the parking lot. As for the remark about the Toyota, the first man had probably noticed my car keys on the table and had decided to scare me.

Before leaving The Point, I spoke with Vuyokazi to check on how she was doing. She agreed that the men had been horrible to her, but she seemed unaware of the *contretemps* that followed. I had also gone to see the club manager, John Justus, to lay a complaint. Justus, a small wiry man with the harried, affable air of someone in customer service, greeted me on the stairs with a reassuring grin. He seemed already to be aware of what had happened. He said he had met the men on the way out and had spoken with them. He was friendly, rueful, conciliatory, as if at an unfortunate misunderstanding. As if the whole thing could be sorted out amicably. The second man, my main abuser, seemed to be someone known to him. Strangely he did not seem to think he was a bad fellow. In fact, he said with a confiding grin, this man and I had pretty much the same first name. (What on earth did he mean?) Anyway, I told myself, the club was on it, it would all be sorted out.

But I was unsettled. All my senses spoke of peril. What was going on? The second man's disproportionate reaction, his refusal to accept an apology, and above all his ice-cold, feral viciousness—all seemed beyond reason. Something from another world had suddenly broken through into the sunlit spaces of my morning. I was thrown off balance.

I was also indignant. I recall arriving at work later that morning and telling colleagues about the huge man who had threatened me. They were shocked and sympathetic. I recall posting a version of what had happened on Facebook. A quick visit to Virgin Active's website had made it clear that the behaviour of the two men was a flagrant violation of club policy: threatening statements and abuse could get you expelled, and taking pictures of other members was also out of bounds. This was not OK!

I emailed a detailed account of the confrontation to John Justus. I wanted him to take action. I asked him to ensure that I could enjoy the club facilities without fear of physical harm. I asked him to enforce his club's rules against these members. And I asked him to provide me with their names so that I would be able to get a restraining order to ensure my safety.

Before the end of the day Justus wrote back. As he had advised earlier, he said, the club would follow its normal process. He promised to keep me informed about any future development.

He did not provide me with the names of the men.

I recall going to the Sea Point police station that evening. The police station was just across a sports field from the club, which now seemed shrouded in a nimbus of vague danger. I sat at a counter in the dimly lit SAPS Customer Service Centre and dictated a detailed statement (a necessary step for securing a restraining order). I recall the black policewoman who took down my account. Initially somewhat nonplussed and amused by my tale of racism and sudden incivility (repeating choice bits of my statement to her colleagues in isiXhosa), she soon seemed to become bored and even irritated by the detail with which I reported every threat, every swearword.

I recall meeting Jay after the visit to the police station, at a modish eatery in Main Road, Sea Point. It was a hot, raucous summer evening. I was unnerved, jumpy. The streets rang with the over-amplified exhausts of passing motorbikes and the shouts of drunken revellers. Underneath its smooth hipster surface the restaurant suddenly felt sleazy and dangerous.

Days passed without any word from management at The Point. Eventually, after several unanswered emails, I visited the club again to meet with Justus and Isak Labuschagne, the Virgin Active regional manager. The Toyota remark had unnerved me, so I took an Uber. I tried to ignore feelings of danger and unease as I entered the club. Everything was just as it had been before, with the clink of weightlifting machines and the tinny rattle of pop music on the speakers. No trace of the Powder Blue brigade. Justus had assured me that the two men would not be there—they had been temporarily banned from the club while management figured out what to do.

I recall perching on a chrome and faux leather chair in Justus's little office. The atmosphere was awkward. Labuschagne and Justus shared chummy, apologetic smiles. They had spoken, they said, to "the guys". They had impressed upon them the seriousness of what they had done. They had warned them very strictly never ever to do anything like this again. I could rest assured that I could use the club facilities without fear of a repeat offence.

They were sorry, but they could not tell me who the men were.

I told them that I was not satisfied. A mere warning from the club was not enough. It did not put me in a position where I could be assured of undisturbed enjoyment of their club facilities. How could I be assured of my safety? And what about my safety outside the club? They looked uncomfortable but they did not change their position, other than to indicate that I would of course be free to pursue my restraining order.

What was going on? Surely, I asked, the men's behaviour was an open and shut case? Why not expel them? Justus put it to me that in his view the men had been provoked. He had talked with them, and they had said that the reason they had been angry was that they felt they had been accused of being racist. This was unfair. Apparently, Justus said, the men worked together in a local business that offered employment to lots of black people.

At this Labuschagne piped up. He said that what had decided the case for him was the fact that they had spoken to another witness. (Who? Powder Blue Three, who had been watching events from a nearby table?) This person had confirmed that he too had had the impression that I had in fact been calling the men racist.

I pushed a bit more. So what? I asked. If the men had disagreed with me, they could have said so in a civil manner. There was no need for them to act in the way they did!

To this, neither Justus nor Labuschagne had a response.

I recall sitting in the windy sunlight outside the club after the meeting, waiting for my Uber home. I was feeling queasy. Something was amiss. This was not going the way I had imagined. Justus and Labuschagne seemed intent on sweeping the matter under the carpet. What was going on?

I wrote another email, and this time copied it to Ross Faragher-Thomas, the Virgin Active CEO. I wanted to inform the company, I said, that I did not regard a mere warning to the men who had threatened me a satisfactory defence of my rights as a club member. Given that the club had failed to intervene in the first place, allowing one of the men to spit in my face in full view of other members, I had no reason to believe that they had the capacity or the means to control their behaviour in future, or to protect me from further harassment. I questioned their failure to act against the men in spite of the fact that they had flagrantly violated club rules. I gave them 24 hours to provide me with full written reasons for their failure to act. "In the absence of any explanation to the contrary," I wrote, "I have no option but to believe that you think their actions were in fact acceptable or defensible."

The next day Justus wrote back, repeating his assurance that the men had been warned not to repeat their behaviour and confirming that Virgin Active management had acted to enforce their rules. But he also said this:

"This was indeed a regrettable incident that took place in our club *during which all parties acted in a manner that gave rise to conflict* [my emphasis]."

I wrote back, expressing puzzlement. What did he mean, all parties? Were they saying I contributed to the conflict? If so, how? I had posed a concern in a civil way. The men could have responded civilly. But they chose not to do so. Could they please explain which of my actions merited such an abusive response on their part?

Justus did not respond.

A word about the times

Before I tell you what happened next, I need to take a step back. Because the events I am recounting, and also the meaning of these events—how they landed on me, and what they left me with—were shaped by those times; by what was going on around me. And shaped also by who I was—or who I thought I was; who I was trying to be, what I thought I was trying to do.

How far back?

I do not know. I am following a thread here.

Perhaps I can begin like this: this, you must understand, was early 2016. Before Brexit, before Trump. Zuma was still president. Before Covid. A different world. A different time. The time before the time we are in now.

Change was coming. Race and rage were in the air.

Just a month before, a Durban-based estate agent called Penny Sparrow had shot to national prominence for writing a social media post in which she had compared black beachgoers to monkeys. The news post spread like wildfire, and Sparrow had suddenly found herself catapulted to notoriety. The previous year, in the middle class suburb of Kenilworth, a white man, a swimming coach called Tim Osrin, had stopped his car to physically assault in broad daylight a black domestic worker, Cynthia Joni, who had been peacefully walking down the road. Osrin's account was that he had thought her to be a sex worker. (It turned out that another woman, a real sex worker this time, accused this man of sexual assault but people made less fuss about her.)

And so it went. Sparrow, Osrin and others like them had swiftly become, somewhat to their own surprise, celebrities of a new kind: they had become poster children for the intuition that beneath the polite and harmonious surface of South African society ugly currents of racial hatred and antagonism still circulated. The days of the 2010 FIFA World Cup, when it had still been possible to be optimistic, or at least cautiously hopeful, about the prospects of our government delivering growth, stability and "a better life for all", were gone. It was no longer possible to even pretend that racism was something that could be relegated to the past. Its festering sores were all around us.

There was a new sense abroad in public life of danger, of skating on thin ice. Was it even possible to call oneself a South African? If you were white, where did you stand? And if you were black, whom could you trust? Iqbal Survé's IOL media company, always ready for a bit of performative politics, had launched a campaign, hash-tagged "#racismstopswithme", calling citizens to take a "personal stand" against "the scourge of racism". Social networks were awash with accusations and counteraccusations. The national fabric, if there ever had been such a thing, was frayed around the edges. Public debate was becoming polarised and rancorous. The shine had well and truly been worn off the surface of our rainbow nation.

Something was ending.

In a way, this was a relief.

Part 2

Cradock

IT'S A WINTER MORNING ON my grandfather's smallholding just outside Cradock. June 1974, or thereabouts. After years of being the headmaster-in-residence of the Afrikaans gymnasium in town, my grandfather has retired here, to a small patch of land just west of the Great Fish River, right next to the railway line running down from Noupoort to Port Elizabeth. At night you can hear the freight train come through slow and huge and heavy; more than a kilometre long, my grandfather says, hauling manganese ore down from the mines in Kimberley. He is very proud of this achievement of our nation. On the other side of the river and the railway line is what my grandparents call "the location", the African township. Later I will understand that this township, Lingelihle, is significant in its own way: it is home to Matthew Goniwe, Fort Calata, Sicelo Mhlauli and Sparrow Mkonto, the anti-Apartheid activists who, ten years from now, will come to be known as the Cradock Four. Men remembered, in other words, for the manner of their deaths, for being detained and then murdered by the South African Police.

But at this point, nine years old, I am unaware of the nature of the world I am growing up in. I do not understand why my mother does not want my uncle to teach me how to shoot. I do not understand why my grandfather's deployment of convict labour on the farm is such an issue for my parents. I do not understand why, when I approach the little shanties where my grandfather's workers live (he refers to them as his *volk*), they do not want to play with me but instead throw little pebbles at me with deadly accuracy.

This morning I am in the garden, next to my grandmother's carefully cultivated patch of rose bushes. It is bitterly cold. The sky is pale blue-grey, and frost covers the rough grass below the *stoep*. My grandfather has assembled his workers in the yard in front of the barn. He is haranguing them. Someone left a farm gate open the evening before, and the cattle got into a neighbour's lucerne.

From where I stand, I recognise two things. I know this habit of my grandfather's: his way of ranting on and on in a voice filled with impotent exasperation. The second is that the workers are just waiting for him to stop. Exactly as I have often done when I have been on the receiving end of these monologues. A group of black men standing sullenly in their threadbare clothes in the winter cold: mute, their breath forming a silent cloud above their heads, their eyes fixed on the ground, while he talks and talks and talks and talks and talks.

In that moment I do not see much more than the fact of their resentful endurance, but in later years my memory returns again and again to this scene. It becomes a moment from which I date a certain awareness, a sense of experiencing the world as being in the process of splitting apart. In which I see a chasm opening, or understand that it has always been there: not mentioned, not spoken of, not named, but there: unbridgeable.

The Koo Valley

I RECALL ANOTHER WINTER NIGHT, more than 20 years later. It was June 1995. I was in the Koo Valley, not far from Montagu. I was there to do fieldwork for a project on legal literacy among farm workers and the role of workers' advice offices in the defence of labour rights.

At that time, NGOs and policy organisations concerned with the harsh lives and appalling working conditions experienced by farm workers on South African farms tended to take a pedagogic approach, assuming that labour justice required that farm workers "know their rights"; that, in other words, what was needed was an enormous education and training project. There was a lot of funding for that kind of thing: the kroner and the pounds were just rolling in, inspired, no doubt, by the clear psychodrama inherent in this cause; a drama of victims and persecutors—on the one side, powerless black farm workers, on the other their racist white oppressors. And, in the middle of it all, the trade unions and NGOs, the defenders of human rights, of simple decency, intervening to set matters straight.

My colleague Steven Robins and I were coming at it from a very different direction: what if, instead of just seeing farm workers as victims of circumstances beyond their control, we were to approach them as resourceful social agents? What skills and strategies did they make use of in their everyday dealings with their white managers and overseers? What were the repertoires of action they could draw on? How did farm workers themselves understand their situation? In other words, what if, instead of assuming that they needed rescuing through "education", we tried to understand their world view in its own right? They, after all, had been dealing with white farmers and the structures of white supremacy for more than three hundred years. Surely any attempt to make things better needed to begin by connecting with the cultural knowledge, the survival strategies, the moral worldviews, of farm workers themselves?

Much to my exasperation, the organisations that claimed to represent farm workers' interests and the unions who sought to mobilise them seemed to me at the time quite uninterested in this question. They seemed to approach farm workers as victims, as backward, servile *lumpens* without class consciousness, people who had to be brought into the fold of the proper workers' struggle as led by COSATU and its member unions, organisations that at that time were seeking to impose on the complex, brutal, intimate world of the farmyard their own bureaucratic model of farm worker organisation, born in urban-based factories in the formal sector.

So this is what we were in the Koo Valley to do: to visit the local farms, to find out how things worked in this poor and far-flung corner of the Western Cape's fruit and canning industry.

Earlier, we had met with the manager of one of these farms, Jacques K, a plain-spoken, jovial white man who answered our questions in his cluttered living room, speaking cheerfully while his wife silently yanked a comb through their daughter's tangled hair. These people do not have money, I thought to myself. I liked Jacques. He struck me as a fair employer—he paid well above the average in the valley, and the farm was a member of the local chapter of the Rural Foundation, a reformist development organisation cautiously introducing fruit and wine farmers to the methods and practices of "enlightened" farm management. There was a workers' representative committee on the farm, and in the previous year, at their instigation, he had spent a large sum of money on the workers' housing, repairing roofs that had been leaking. They had also built a community hall for the workers with a colour TV. He assented easily to our request to interview the workers, and even offered to set up the interviews there and then. Steven and I politely declined. We would contact the workers ourselves; all we needed was for him to let them know that they had his permission to speak to us. We agreed to return on Friday afternoon, when the workday was over.

By the time we got back to the farm the sun had gone. A storm had moved through the valley the night before, but the sky had cleared. The air was heavy and dense and cold in that way it has in the heart of the Western Cape winter. The ground and trees were sopping wet; the silent sky above was thronged with stars. There were no lights. In the dark we could not find the shed that contained the farm shop. Eventually we stumbled into a row of farm workers' houses. We knocked on the first door; a woman answered.

Inside, the house was gloomy, candlelit. No radio playing. No electricity. A smoky fire was burning in the hearth. I had an eerie sense that we had gone back in time a hundred and fifty years, as if the memory of slavery was still present, still felt. Behind the woman a little girl looked on wide-eyed at the white men who had unexpectedly appeared outside. I thought involuntarily of Vron Ware, writing about Whiteness as racial terror. What could our presence mean to this little girl? Could it spell anything but trouble? Her mother knew about the meeting, though, and quietly explained to us which way to go.

We found the workers in a circle at the farm shop, a single spotlight glaring into our eyes and illuminating their overcoats and caps. The atmosphere was relaxed, and Jacques joked with the men as he handed out the 12.5 kg bags of flour, salt and bottles of "fish oil", which is what Western Cape working class people call the sunflower oil used for cooking. Acting on an intuition, we did not come up to him or greet him; we simply slipped silently into the outskirts of the circle and waited. "These are the guys I have told you about, Jacques said. They want to meet you in the community hall. Tell them whatever you want to, speak freely." There was a murmur of assent.

The community hall was a bare brick structure with a concrete floor. They had built it themselves, the workers told us. It was their space. There was an old TV and a couple of benches. There was a heater and a single, bare, electric light. All the workers were there, as well as many family members, everyone sitting along the walls—arranged, we noted, in strict order of seniority, with the oldest men right by the heater, then the women, and the children sitting quietly at the furthest edges, more interested in the TV than in us.

What I remember about the conversation was the quiet intensity of it, and the bitter anger of the men who spoke to us. If we had met at the manager's offices, or if we had met in daytime, or if management had directly invited the workers, we would have heard a different story. But tonight we tapped into another layer, another current of feeling, a different truth. It was not that Jacques K had lied to us when he had painted the rosy picture of labour relations on his farm and listed the various things he had put in place to help "uplift the community". All those things were true. He did in fact pay significantly better than other farmers. He did not use violence. He had, in fact, made money and building materials available and had supported the building of the community centre. You could work with him, the men said; he was, they said—using a formulation familiar to me from my research on farm worker discourse—a man you could "understand". That was all true. But this did not change the fact that he was up there, in his brightly-lit warm house, that his wife would at this very moment be filling his bath with hot water ready on tap, while they and their wives would have to scavenge in the dark for firewood; that they would work their whole lives long and have nothing to show for it; that he, like any white manager, *gee maar net om dat die werk gedoen word* (only cared about the work being done); that he did not *see* them; that his voice counted as theirs did not.

Did they think anything would change, I asked, now that Mandela was free, now that a new government was in power?

They did not think so.

What was remarkable about that evening for me was not what was said, but that it was sayable. For our entire stay in

Montagu and all the other hamlets we had visited, Steven and I had been constantly aware of the extent to which everyone we met—white and black, workers and managers—kept within the limits of a carefully laundered presentation of Western Cape rural reality; a discourse about "transformation", about the need for "development" and "upliftment", about the good intentions of all involved—a discourse so uniform that in interview after interview, we could almost predict the words. The most farm workers would say to us when we spoke to them was the same formulaic phrase: *die boer is nie sleg nie maar die geld is te min* (the farmer is not too bad but the money is too little).

We suspected strongly that this was not the whole truth; that alongside this anodyne presentation of reality another realm existed, a realm Steven and I, in our running conversations, dubbed the Western Cape's "black underground"; the world that the anarchist political theorist James C Scott called the "hidden transcript", the "offstage" spaces where anger, disillusionment, disagreement and "resistance" could be voiced, and where the cultural memories of slavery, subaltern life and dreams of defiance could be transmitted. Thus far we had only suspected its existence. Tonight, somehow—perhaps because we were meeting with the workers in their own space, perhaps because we had communicated a level of openness and respect that made them feel safe to share their thoughts, perhaps because we had not publicly associated ourselves with the manager in the circle at the shop—we had broken through the deceptive meniscus of rural social life to hear a different voice.

But what was this anger? What could it achieve? Two things struck Steven and me about what passed between the workers and us on that winter's night. The first was just how close to the surface— *and how hidden from sight*—the undercurrents of the "black underground" ran. The workers who sat around us complaining about their treatment were the very same ones who had laughed and joked with Jacques K only minutes before—and who still genuinely characterised him, despite the harshness of their lives, as a good boss. Yet they had given us a completely different perspective on their lives, giving vent to the desperation that circulated beneath.

The second was how much the way in which these workers spoke to us diverged from the standard forms of "worker consciousness" imagined by trade unionists, activists and NGOs. It was not a language of public power and of class struggle but of bitter awareness of injustice unallayed. It was not, nor did it yet seem to be, an anger that could speak its name, that could *address* the manager, that could be a vehicle for a meaningful encounter between his world—the unreflective power of the master—and the one they inhabited.

Could it be fashioned into such a vehicle? I had no doubt that it could. But it seemed to me that if it would ever be, it would look and sound very different from the ready-made slogans of workers' unity, of "knowing your rights", and of state intercession and bureaucratic recognition that dominated the discourse of the farm worker NGO sector at the time.

I did not know what to do with what the workers told me. But I felt that we had been entrusted with something; with the possibility of hope, perhaps. Or just with the duty to bear witness.

After the meeting we walked out with some of the workers, who accompanied us to Steve's pickup truck. My back muscles were aching from the cold. I thought guiltily about the warm bed and supper that awaited us.

Among those who accompanied us was the woman who had met us in the candlelit house. Her little girl was in her arms. She was a tiny little thing, not quite four years old. A beautiful child, with shining dark eyes and a soft cloud of curly hair. She saw the pen that I was putting away in my shoulder bag—a favourite of mine, a shiny steel fountain pen with a calligraphic nib that I had bought in the UK the year before. She held out her hands. I gave it to her. She clutched it tightly. *Gee terug die pen vir die man*, the mother said (give back the pen to the man). It looks like she wants it, I told her. She does not know what to do with it, the mother replied. Maybe she wants to write, I said. She must learn to write! The child silently held the pen out for me to take back. I felt the weight of the centuries and the spirits of the dead like a swirling cloud around us. Where was this child heading? What would her future be? Would she follow in her mother's footsteps? Or would she know a different life? Gently I took the pen from her hands, and we headed back into the dark.

Wivenhoe

ANOTHER WINTER NIGHT: DECEMBER 1994, the previous year. I was in the final stages of my PhD. This was in Wivenhoe, a village not far from the campus of Essex University, a quiet little hamlet where postgraduate students rented rooms and living space. A few months before, my partner Zimitri and I had found a little boatshed right on the river Colne that had been converted to living quarters. Zimitri had gone back to South Africa, taking a job at the Department of Sociology at the University of Cape Town. I'd stayed on, working on the final chapters of my dissertation.

This night I was cooking supper for a fellow student in our PhD programme, Barnor Hesse. Barnor was black and British, formidably intellectual, self-possessed and grave, a protégé of Stuart Hall and Paul Gilroy, who were at that time among the foremost left-wing intellectuals in the UK. Two years before, Barnor had shocked me by walking out of a seminar I had been giving on the power relations between farm workers and farm owners. Before departing, he had taken me to task about what appeared to be a curious silence in my work: the fact that in all my arguments and discussions, I did not even once mention that the workers I had been describing were black. Neither did I mention, confront, or think about the implications of the fact that I was white. What did that mean for the nature of the interactions between me and my informants? What did that mean for the nature of the story I was telling? And what were the reasons for my apparent inability to "mark the space I speak from"?

Odd as it may seem now, these were indeed questions to which I had not given much thought at all. They had not been part of the discourse, the mental universe, of anti-Apartheid struggle back in the late 1980s and early 1990s. But I could see that they were important questions, and I tried my best to answer them even as Barnor and some of his fellow students packed their bags and prepared to leave. Have you got any advice for me, any suggestions about how to address this problem? I had asked somewhat desperately, as Barnor headed for the exit. No. My project, he replied from the door, was not salvageable. It was too irredeemably shaped by complicity with Apartheid's racism.

Since that somewhat unpromising first meeting, Barnor had changed, and so had I. We had become, if not friends, at least partners in a complex, delicate, and for me quite charged conversation. I needed, I had come to see, to learn to unlearn, to figure out how to be white, or how not to be—or, at least, how to be white in a different way; how to find a way to climb down from the distant pinnacle of unreflective privilege from which my modes of knowing and speaking about the world had been shaped. I was, I felt, seeking a track down from Mount Olympus, trying to find a way of speaking and writing that was situated *in* the world, not gazing down at it from above, objective and neutral. And Barnor had done me the singular honour of being willing and able to address me, and in so doing to help me find my way.

Hence this supper—a last conversation before I headed back to South Africa. I recall Barnor's patience, his gentleness; his implacable and probing questions. Over dessert (he refused wine but sipped politely at my proffered pot of Rooibos tea) he asked me, Andries, what changed? What prompted you to take this path, from being so blind, so self-assured, so unconscious, so loudly and stridently *deaf* two years ago, to being more open, more willing to listen, to learn? Well, I said, there is the small fact of my relationship with Zimitri. Being in a relationship with a black woman, herself on a journey of consciousness and discovery, is a powerful antidote to the blind spots and the smugness of non-racial and unthinking white male privilege. Barnor acknowledged that, but he still wanted to know: what had changed? What accounted for my willingness to engage with this path?

I said to him that it related to his charge of complicity the year before. It was not an accusation I could deny. It was clear to me that the response of so many liberal and left-wing whites (*actually I am not like the rest of them*) would not wash. That was a lie. I was indeed complicit. I *was* part of the structures of privilege. There was no denying it or getting away from it. All I could do was *own* my complicity, accept it, take responsibility for it, and then see what was possible from there on; to see if it was still possible to step into relationship or conversation. To find ways of hearing others, and being heard.

Barnor seemed to assent to this. The question, he said, was to find out whether there are ways of encountering each other that are not predetermined by the past, that are not defined by the shadow of, as he put it, "this giant that doth bestride us all".

I liked that.

Before the evening ended, Barnor asked me a question. We had been discussing the nature of the structures of white privilege. Publicly challenging and debating these things was one thing, he pointed out. But what, he wanted to know, did I think my response would be if I encountered racism, or unconscious white privilege, in my private life? What if I was at a dinner party, among other white people, and a friend of mine said something objectionable or unconscious? Smiling ironically, he quoted to me the words of Jesus to Peter at the Last Supper. What will you say if no witnesses are present? *Wilt thou then disown me?*

I don't recall what I answered, but I never forgot that question.

Part 3

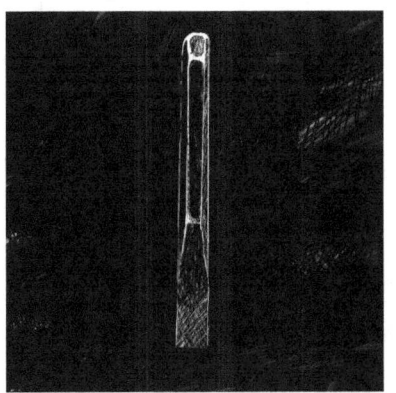

Critique in the world

I AM A WHITE MALE South African. Middle class. Eldest son, *only* son—that's crown prince status right there—in an Afrikaans family. My grandfather had been a headmaster; my father a university professor; my mother had been a teacher like her mother before her. Half my uncles were *dominees* in the Dutch Reformed Church. But we had broken with our tribe. (It was, I believe, my mother who radicalised us: as a young woman in the late 1950s, teaching in the coloured schools around Stellenbosch, she had befriended some of her colleagues who, as far as I can make out, must have been members of the Unity Movement; jazz lovers, critical, committed to teaching and thinking as a pathway to liberation.) So I grew up in an anti-Apartheid household in Stellenbosch in the 1970s and 1980s, in the heartland of Nationalist ideology, in the belly of the beast, born into a tightly knit, dissident subculture of left and liberal Afrikaners. Orphan children of the Enlightenment. My family had left the Dutch Reformed Church, appalled at its complicity with Apartheid, but I think all of us inherited something of the church's Protestant moralism, its concern with rectitude and being right—with being *in* the right.

    I grew up a bookish boy, in love with letters and the life of the mind; freaked out by the undercurrent of violence and inhumanity that seethed around the protected bubble of our university town. Not knowing where I stood, where I belonged, not knowing how to locate myself in what was going on around me. I did not fit in at school—bookish boys were not treated kindly at Paul Roos Gymnasium—but where *did* I fit in? As a schoolboy, enamoured of science fiction and fantasy, I identified not with the starship troopers at war with alien hordes, but with poor King Arthur in TH White's *The Once and Future King*, trying to avert the battle, caught in the middle of the ruinous clash between his warring beloveds.

And somewhere along the way—somewhere between the ages of 16 and 20, I think—I had concluded that what I needed to do was to *understand* things. I don't want to oversimplify matters here or project a simple formula back into the past. But I know that I derived a sense of safety, of reprieve from roiling feelings and the ever-present threat of choking depression from being able to grasp things in my mind. Mastering them by *describing* them. Delving in my father's stacks of paperbacks I had come across James Baldwin's *The Fire Next Time* and somehow gleaned from it a sense of how writing could be a way of grasping thoughts that would otherwise slide by unremarked; a way of taking a fiery chaos of feelings and making something beautiful of it. How writing could be a way of making yourself known to yourself—and to the world; a way of *making* a self, of becoming someone.

During my university education, I had been schooled in a strand of philosophical thought that called itself critical theory. It is an offshoot of 18th century Western enlightenment thought, reaching us through patrilineal descent via Marx, Freud and Foucault—a tradition that links the striving for social justice and a good society to the critical investigation of the hidden structures that underpin everyday life in capitalism. It is a way of thinking that is suspicious of the ordinary, taken-for-granted surface of liberal industrial society. Where others see progress, rationality, common sense and freedom, it attends to conflict, to antagonism, and to the way the smooth veneer of normal life is belied and shaped by relationships of power. It is, truth be told, an odd tradition; one which is fairly obscure, intellectually specialised, deeply scholarly—but which at the same time holds, in Karl Marx's famous phrase, that the point is not merely to understand the world, but to change it. Understanding the world *to* change it; changing the world *by* understanding it. This was my lodestar, the story I told myself as I tried to find my way.

So that's how I came to get that PhD. Partly it was because university study was the only way in which I could get deferment of military conscription. Studying overseas was a way to escape being sucked into the violence and cruelty that was engulfing South Africa, even if it led to the bleak possibilities and difficult choices of exile. (Exile, to be frank, was where I thought I was headed in those days.)

But partly I was also in search of tools that could help me make sense of the world. The smug certitude and blindness of South African liberalism had long irked me, but I had become disillusioned, too, with the bullying moralism and paranoid self-righteousness of South African communists and their impatience with troublesome thoughts or questions that did not fit into the self-serving version of history being bruited about by the Congress movement. There was every sign that, in the unlikely event of the ANC seizing power, they would simply re-arrange the cruel structures of colonialism, doing away with formal racial discrimination while reserving for themselves the seats at the high table of inequality. For a while my friends and I had flirted with the remnants of Western Cape Trotskyism and academic Marxism. But for me that, too, palled: it was a self-contained and stultifying creed, stuck in the bitterness of being right about the past, captured in its own circular narrative. It was a theology, a doctrine; not a tool for understanding the world.

And this was not just an academic matter. I absolutely needed such tools. In my mid-twenties I had become involved at the periphery of the anti-Apartheid struggle: in my spare time, as a volunteer in a legal advice office seeking to defend the rights of the farm workers that lived in inhuman conditions on the beautiful wine farms all around my hometown; and as part of the war resistance movement, as a conscientious objector to Apartheid's military conscription. One of the most important things I had learned in both those processes was that the existing categories of political thought, the ways in which both "liberals" and "radicals" spoke about and explained the frightening, ambiguous, endlessly shifting reality around me were simply not helpful; providing moralising narratives where discernment was needed, imposing crude categories where reality seemed fluid.

Hence that boatshed in Wivenhoe. I embarked on a PhD reading poststructuralist discourse analysis, and signed up to write a dissertation on the power relations between black farm workers and white farmers. But I registered not in South Africa but, of all places, Essex University in the UK, and I chose as my supervisor the Argentinian political theorist Ernesto Laclau. Ernesto, along with Chantal Mouffe, had written *Hegemony and Socialist Strategy*, at the time celebrated as a manifesto for a new form of radical democratic politics, a project that broke decisively with the dead end of orthodox Marxism.

This turned out to have been not altogether a bad move. I was fascinated by the sophistication and reach of the concepts and ideas that were being discussed by Ernesto and his students. In their emphasis on the open-textured nature of political reality, the indeterminacy and potential fluidity of the social fabric, in the notion that social identity and social reality were things *made*, not *given*, Ernesto and Chantal's ideas seemed to be a way of thinking that was open to *not knowing*, to the emergence of new possibilities, to novel ways of thinking and doing, to things not already predicted by the comfortable ideological and moral certitudes of the warring ideologies that dominated South African political life.

But I was also alienated by the arid intellectualism of poststructuralist academia. Ernesto and many of my fellow students seemed disdainful of the complexity of the real world and the boring details of actual politics. Our seminars seemed at times to sink into self-indulgent obscurantism. "What is this 'thinking' that can truly be called 'thinking?'" asked Rodolphe Gasché, a sweet and charming man visiting us at a colloquium about Deconstruction and Politics in 1995. He fixed us with his mild and penetrating gaze and obliged us with the answer: "It is the thinking of that impossible *possible*-Impossible". Well, there you have it.

This was not for me. I took from Ernesto and his disciples what I could, but when I returned home from my PhD I chose to look for a job, not in a traditional academic department, but in the field of policy research.

Because the world had changed. In the middle of my postgraduate years, Nelson Mandela had been released from prison and the ANC had been unbanned. Instead of heading uncertainly into exile, flying away from a society locked in an inescapable doom loop, I could return. Instead of existing in the unthinkable never-never of an impossible future revolution, democracy was suddenly a practical reality, something that was being invented all around us. Post-Apartheid South Africa was not a fantasy but something that needed to be built, right now.

So that is what I did. I came home. I met a man called Ben Cousins who was starting a new land reform policy research outfit, the Programme for Land and Agrarian Studies, at the University of the Western Cape, and I talked him into giving me a job. And I never left. PLAAS has been my professional, political and intellectual home ever since.

The chisel

It is hard to explain what it was like to be a researcher, a "policy expert", during those two first decades of life in the newly democratic South Africa. It was an exciting place to be, very different from the work on offer in a normal teaching department. Our job was to do rigorous, high quality social science research on some of the burning questions of our time: how to resolve South Africa's "land question", how to transform the exploitative relations on commercial farms, how to reduce or eradicate poverty. Here were opportunities to do research that could directly shape the path of social change!

But often those opportunities turned out to be oddly circumscribed and limited. You had to be careful. This was not really a surprise. We had just come out of a civil war. The wounds were everywhere, raw and festering. Mistrust, too. It was an ambiguous time; hopeful and optimistic, even—but accompanied by a strong sense that hope depended on not pushing too hard against the polite and bland surface of everyday life. You were not supposed to look too deep or ask too many questions.

Think about it like this: racism and the ineluctable consequences of racialized identity had been part of the warp and weft of everyday life. What you could do, what you could think, what you could say, had for three centuries been circumscribed with iron certainty by your place in society, by what you were, by what you were taken to be. Identity was destiny. It was in our bones. It had simply been part of everybody's understanding of how the world worked. Everybody had been steeped in it.

And then, just like that, by universal consensus, all that had been banished, as if it had never been. Ways of thinking that had been taken for granted were now unthinkable—or at least had to be earnestly disavowed. From one moment to the next, the embattled language of the state of emergency, of a battle without compromise to an unimaginable end, gave way to the upbeat discourse of rainbow unity. The broadcasts of the SABC, until just a year before a bastion of the fight against communism, now resounded to the childlike strains of "*Simunye—we are one!*"

All without missing a beat, as if *this* was who we had been all along, as if we had been doing it forever. As if everything that had happened before had been a bad dream.

But if we had wakened from a nightmare, it was a nightmare that, it seemed, we should perhaps not think about too deeply, lest it wake again and engulf us all once more. I kept thinking, at the time, of the Ravenous Bugblatter Beast of Traal in Douglas Adams's *The Hitchhiker's Guide to the Galaxy*. This is a monster that believes that as long as *you* can't see *it*, *it* can't see *you*; so that the thing to do in its presence is to always *look very carefully away*. Those days are often remembered as giddily optimistic, hopeful. But it was also a time in which pools of silence collected at the edges.

So it was, too, in my new job as a policy researcher. While the world was awash in resources for those who wished to do good work, the funds available to do this work came with strings attached and were often shaped by unstated agendas. The Cold War had ended. The complex geopolitics of anti-colonial struggles had made way for a new, one-size-fits all project—"development", with its cargo of shiny buzzwords and portable solutions. The organisation once known as the British Colonial Office was now rebranded the Department for International Development (DFID). The frameworks that we had developed to understand anti-colonial struggles were gone in a flash, replaced by discourses of policy deliberation that had implicit rules and silences of their own.

It was a thoroughly technocratic world, constructed around anodyne, upbeat goals (broad-based growth! social inclusion! food security! stakeholder involvement!) with little patience to engage with the challenging realities of antagonism, ambiguity, racism, conflict, or contention. We needed simple, implementable answers. ("Tell me your research findings about chronic poverty in South Africa," a DFID mandarin asked me one day at a conference in Manchester, "but for God's sake don't tell me it's *complicated*.") Elaborately crafted problem statements turned out to be focused away from the areas where the real difficulties lay. The areas of consensus upon which our work depended turned out to conceal deep and unstated areas of disagreement. You could be part of the important conversations—as long as you agreed to ignore certain uncomfortable facts.

For me, this work provoked an odd sense of disconnection. My PhD had been my entrance ticket to this world. It was my licence. It was the basis upon which I was able to present myself as an "expert", as someone entitled to bid for funding, to be part of the conversation, someone with authority and knowledge. But I could never, ever, actually *use* the particular skills and tools that I had acquired during my intellectual training. Marxist class analysis was out of bounds. Critical race theory—yes, it was a thing even in those days—was not seen as a useful tool; it was something for people in departments of literature to worry about. As for poststructuralist discourse analysis, you must be joking. Even South African leftists frowned on that stuff.

Recently Yanis Varoufakis, trying to convey the way in which these closed worlds of policy deliberation worked, called it the Adults in the Room syndrome. As he tells it, you had to choose. You could be an insider, one of the "grownups", part of the conversations that shape the compromises by which society is ruled and policies are made, but bound to complicity and silence about them. Or you could be outside, powerless. He chose to leave.

At PLAAS, we tried something different. What we did was what one of my colleagues came to call "chameleoning". You appeared to accept the language in which proposals, funding, and research projects were couched. Making Markets Work for the Poor. Promoting Social Inclusion. Policies for Inclusive Growth. Strengthening Women's Rights in Land. But you also pushed back against it. You contested it. You took the bland and technocratic language of the time—the Millennium Development Goals, "poverty alleviation", "food security", "evidence-based policy" (even, I kid you not, "evidence based *research*")—and you tried to bend it to new purposes, so that some part of what was unsaid could be said, so that real work could be done, useful conversations could be had.

So when I say I felt I had to put aside the tools that I had acquired during my PhD training, I am not being entirely accurate. I had learned something during those years. I had learned to trust my doubts and to follow hunches. I had learned to recognise the feeling in my gut when a problem statement, or an explanation, or the smooth and compelling normative narratives of policy-speak felt "off", felt wrong, felt false.

And I had learned to use writing. I had learned how to articulate a vague sense of unease, how to put the words on paper and then see where they took me. Not quite "following an argument where it leads"—that makes it sound too logical, too linear. Following a hunch, an intuition, following an elusive trail, a blood spoor through dense bush. And by feeling ahead, one word at a time, I could find out what I was thinking and what needed to be said.

In her *Earthsea* series, Ursula K Le Guin describes the art of magic in these terms: witchcraft and wizardry, she says, lie in the ability of the women and men who practice it to find the true names of things. If you can find the right words, if you can *name* something, then you can exert your power over it. Without it, power can't get traction.

It is a compelling and beautiful idea. But with time I have come to feel that it is not quite like that. It is less like *naming* and more like *carving*. It's more like trying to open a space in which it is possible to say something worth saying. Perhaps like using the Subtle Knife in Philip Pullman's *Dark Materials* trilogy: the knife that, when wielded with enough sensitivity by one who knows how to use it, can open the portal that connects different worlds.

In his poem, "Die Beiteltjie", the Afrikaans poet NP Van Wyk Louw describes finding "a small, small chisel". A humble little thing. Shiny. It does not look like much. The trick is to know precisely where to put its edge, how to angle it, and then to tap it just so to split the pebble. And then an impermeable rock, a boulder, the whole planet, the universe itself cleaves apart before his eyes in a clean line.

So for a while it was possible to do interesting and worthwhile work. I did research, I wrote articles, and I had a blog of my own (A Subtle Knife, I called it—it is still up, check it out) where I shared my evolving ideas. After fifteen years, Ben Cousins stepped down as director of PLAAS (we still had the same acronym, but now we were the Institute for Poverty, Land and Agrarian Studies) and I took his place at the helm.

Make no mistake: I never stopped feeling somewhat out of place in the bland and edgeless world of development discourse, and I never entirely shook off the feeling that the policy documents I was reading were actually a species of fantasy literature, although with bullet points and infographics rather than dragons and wizards. Neither was I entirely at home in the intellectual world of PLAAS, where most of my colleagues identified as Marxists of one stripe or another. But in the context of the time that was not an issue. What mattered was that we had a broad common purpose—pushing at the limits of the mainstream consensus, trying to keep alive a vision of social justice beyond the narrow limits of established policy. And we were also connected by a strong sense of collegial respect, by a shared commitment to scholarly excellence and practical relevance, by the sense of being part of a close-knit team. So, difficult and frustrating as it sometimes was, I felt lucky. I felt privileged.

I was working.

The comfort of enemies

Let me try to account for where I had arrived by the time 2016 rolled around, how far I had travelled since the day I saw my grandfather through his workers' eyes. What I understood. Or at least what I thought I understood.

Most particularly, and most elusively, this: that if my youthful experience had been of a world tearing itself in two, a world riven right down the centre by a mortal conflict, a world in which all you could do was to choose a side—or worse yet, to accept that the side you found yourself on was the side you should fight for, whether you liked it or not—I was having none of that.

Clearly there was a struggle. But it seemed to me that what I wanted was not victory of one side over another but *resolution*. Not triumph but ... what?

Here's a bit of political theory. One of the things I had learned in my Essex days was that some of the deepest and most fraught divisions in the world around us were not about ethnic and cultural identity (as the Afrikaner Nationalists would have it). Neither were they, as per the liberals, driven either by (rational) competition for resources or (irrational) ideology. Nor yet were they the expression of that wonderful bit of 19th century Hegelian idealism still touted by Marxists today, "social contradictions". Rather, one could think of them as being shaped by what Ernesto and Chantal and their followers would call the articulation of *antagonism*—that is, a relation defined by the fact that *each side defines itself in relation to the threat posed by the other.*

If you look long and hard enough at many seemingly unresolvable social struggles, you find a strange knot of circular reasoning at their heart, a place where the very identity of one side, the basis of its sense of who it is, depends on the construction of the notion of an Enemy which supposedly thwarts it and prevents it from full self-realisation. In Nazi Germany, the fantasy of the parasitic Jew was essential to the very notion of a German people struggling to fulfil its racial identity. The project of articulating and creating a sense of an Afrikaner *volk* required the invention of a panoply of demons (liberals, communists, the *swart gevaar*) in relationship to which the struggle for cultural self-determination was defined. This, said Ernesto, was the paradoxical process at the heart of all political contention. It did not have to be right-wing or destructive. It might also be inspiring, part of the struggle for democracy, the struggle of the people versus its oppressors.

This was useful in many ways, but in the end it left me unsatisfied. In a social field structured by antagonism, there are only "us" and "them"; only the Oppressed and its Others, no possibility of a middle ground not defined by this conflict. Antagonism, as Ernesto was fond of remarking, does not admit of a third term. In Glasgow, a Scottish housemate of mine used to say, even atheists had to declare whether they were Protestant atheists or Catholic atheists. Netanyahu needs Hamas, Hamas needs Netanyahu.

A pox on both their houses! I was interested in something else. Powerful as the notion of antagonism was, and as compelling as the narratives driving polarisation in the world around me were, it was plain that as a way of acting in the world, they required you to oversimplify. As Ernesto had himself pointed out, they depended on a circular argument, a blind spot. You had to flatten the complexity, the ambiguity, the unfinishedness of the world around you; to buy into narratives in which your side was either the victim or the rescuer—at any rate, the one free from blame—while all the cruelty and disappointment could safely be split off and blamed on the compelling and, yes, comforting figure of an enemy who was *not you,* but whose existence secretly provided the anchor for your morally stabilised universe.

Now, clearly no life worth living is lived without adversaries. But what about the *comforting* enemy? What about the enemy whom I profess to hate, but upon whom my sense of self secretly depends? Somewhere beyond all talk of right and wrong, the Sufi mystic Rumi is said to have said: There is a field. I will meet you there.

When I had returned to South Africa in 1995, I had, in one sense, few illusions. Talk about the South African "miracle" seemed false and dishonest. The political settlement was not a miracle: it was a choice borne of desperation. A descent into civil war had been averted, but at a price. Negotiations had been accompanied, not by the cessation but by the intensification of political violence. And some of the most important structures of oppression and privilege had been left intact.

Neither could you call it, as many on the left did, a betrayal. Certainly, many revolutionary promises and ideals had been shelved, but unless you were delusional you had to acknowledge that this was not betrayal but just accommodation to some very harsh realities. And at least this left open the possibility that the work could go on.

But it had to go on in a different way. Ernesto and his coterie liked to focus on "antagonism" because, leftists all, they lived for those moments of disruption, for the volcanic moments when the common people, coming together, shook off their shackles and threw into confusion the neat plans of the bureaucrats. But there was something adolescent about this, something contemptuous of the difficult work of making compromises in the real world. Democratic populism, the project of constructing the identity of "the people" opposed to the oppressive state, had been entirely appropriate in the 1980s when the task had been to make the country ungovernable. But it was poorly suited to thinking about the new challenges, which were all about *governing well*. This is what we now had to find out how to do.

Maybe this was—and perhaps still is—my remaining illusion: That the "new South Africa" might be very much a dream, but it could be a *productive* dream. That good work could be done in its name. That the possibility existed of creating ways of thinking and acting not simply stuck in the predictable ruts of mutual enmity, but rooted in the arduous work of mutual recognition, of acting to create the kindness and solidarity that had not existed before. Making love, as the song said, out of nothing at all.

So in the years after 1995, this was where I found myself again and again. Between the camps. Not because I did not want to choose sides, or believed that conflict should be avoided. But if conflict had turned sterile, if the debates and struggles around us had become stuck, if neither victory nor defeat were possible, something else needed to happen. What if you could reframe the terms of the conflict? What if you could find the third term excluded and denied by simple antagonism, the ground upon which new possibilities, new ways of thinking and acting, could emerge?

You might wonder whether, in some ways, I wasn't still that little boy standing behind the rose bushes, wondering where he belonged in a divided world. Perhaps I was. Perhaps I still am. According to the system of personality typing known as the Enneagram, I am a Type Nine—the "adaptive peacemaker". One of the less useful characteristics of us Nines is that we can be too willing to go along with others to "keep the peace". But I also believe that sometimes it is possible to be not the peacekeeper but the peace*maker*. The bridge builder. To act in the interests of a wholeness that *is not yet evident*, that is in the process of becoming.

And also, I had some tools.

Working

FOR ONE THING, AS WE worked over the years to better understand the causes and implications of persistent poverty and inequality in South Africa, I felt I was able to get something of a handle on what was going wrong, on where the difficulties lay with the society we were constructing, and about why inequality was getting worse, not better. I felt more and more critical of those accounts that were satisfied simply to blame it all on capitalism or on "neoliberalism". Though accurate, of course, in the most general sense, I could not see how such an analysis actually helped anyone, other than to establish the radical credentials of the analyst. Capitalism can be managed in many different ways (in fact, dear reader, I would argue that socialism, properly understood, is essentially just one particular way of managing capitalism). Many of the problems that we have in South Africa are due not to capitalism per se, but to the specific way it has been configured and the policy choices that have been made about how the costs and benefits of capitalist development are distributed. Those policy choices can be changed. Policies can be imagined that would certainly fall far short of "fundamental change" (whatever that means), but which could still make a difference.

What about all the other stuff? What about racism, pain and trauma? What about dealing with all the dreadful baggage we have been saddled with, and which still smoulders away beneath the surface of everyday life? Oddly enough (I can sense Barnor's raised eyebrow here) this was still not something that our

Institute was particularly interested in as a policy problem. We dealt with land, with livelihoods, with inequality, with the basic underlying material realities. As Marxists would put it, with the "base", not the "superstructure". Perhaps there was a sense that if we could make land reform work, the worst legacies of racism would thereby be dealt with.

Neither did we ever pay much detailed and thoughtful attention to the question of our own positionality; to how the history of racial privilege shaped and refracted our ways of being with one another in the office. I suppose that most of the time, our sense of shared political commitment was glue enough. I suspect that being at a "historically black university", where the power structures were not white, also helped. And it seems that some of us (not me!) thought that our political credentials excused us, even those of us who were white, from doing our "race work". The racists were out there: the white farmers, the wealthy capitalists. Not us.

There was a word for this way of thinking. Many years ago the psychologist Carl Gustav Jung had used the term "splitting" to describe the strategy of coping with anxiety and other painful feelings by locating distressing aspects of the self "out there", "projecting" them (to use Freud's term) onto others, allowing the self to reject what it finds aversive and to affirm its own virtue. That, it seemed to me, was what was at play in the addiction to righteous anger I thought I detected in many corners of left-wing academia and politics in South Africa and elsewhere. It seemed to me, for example, to be what drove the tendency to cast so many of those struggling around us – farm workers, small farmers, the poor – as the hapless victims of unfeeling monsters: that moralising victim-persecutor narrative again, a story about ourselves that allowed us to portray ourselves as the noble rescuers, the righteous accusers, the defenders of the weak against the strong.

Things could not go on in this unconscious way forever, I thought. Sooner or later there would have to be a reckoning. In my personal life, I had the good fortune to have plenty of opportunities to continue working at this baggage: for a few years (until we divorced) with Zimitri, who taught me most of what I know both about the psychological impact of racialised experience and the depth and extent of my own blindness. But also in subsequent years, as part of the ManKind Project, a progressive men's network working to support positive models of masculinity, where we white men had no option but to sit in the fire of hearing and feeling the anger of black men and confronting our own unconscious assumptions.

Mostly, I think, I learned what love can do: how much change is possible when people are able to step out of the well-worn ruts of attack and defence, and to meet, not in perfect reconciliation, not in transcendence, but in the painful process of finding ways to speak truth.

By speaking of love, I am not being sentimental. Usually, when people invoke love, they refer to its affective dimensions: the desire for connection, or for the giving and receiving of care or nourishment. Those are indeed important. But love can also be thought of as a particular *stance* towards the Other. This I learned from my friend and mentor Shakti Malan, who helped me find my way through the emotional turmoil I found myself in after the death of my mother and the end of my first marriage. Shakti (aka Liezel, before she chose to change her name to that of the female principle of divine energy herself) was a follower of the Vijñāna Bhairava Tantra, a slender and ancient text teaching the practices and disciplines necessary for the experience and comprehension of the most beautiful and most terrifying aspects of conscious human existence. Love, Shakti used to say, is simply the ability to be utterly present for the Other, to be completely open to them, to be able to hear and see them, and to meet them without reservation wherever they are coming from.

Not an easy thing.

This is why I said, earlier in this essay, that the death of the dream of rainbow nationalism was a relief to me. Perhaps we needed, as a nation, to go through the process of losing hope—if hope was fastened to fantasies of magical redemption. Perhaps the illusions of rainbow nationalism and technocratic progress could make way for something much more difficult but much more fruitful. Perhaps we were entering, I thought, something akin to what the psychoanalyst Melanie Klein had called "the depressive position"—the moment when the patient realises that all their stories have run out, that they have nobody else to blame for all that has gone wrong, that there is no comforting enemy, no disavowed other; there is only us, trying to figure out how to handle with grace and compassion the unholy shitshow around us. To face reality in all its painful beauty and ugliness. That, said Klein, was when the real work could begin.

Part 4

Hexagram 23: "Splitting Apart"

Prominent people

It is 30 September 2015. It's a blustery, cloudy day with a damp north-westerly wind. We are in Jameson Hall, at the University of Cape Town. The dimly lit, cavernous space is half full; not with UCT students or staff, but with members of the Cape Town intelligentsia from all over the peninsula. The event is the 13th Annual Nelson Mandela Lecture, a keystone event in the South African liberal calendar, convened by the Nelson Mandela Foundation to "invite prominent people to drive debate on significant social issues". I managed to secure a ticket, so I guess that makes me a prominent person.

This year's guest is Thomas Piketty. Piketty recently shot to international prominence as the author of *Capital in the Twenty-First Century*, a doorstopper of a book which became a surprise bestseller a couple of years ago. The book itself is not particularly radical but its runaway success has been widely seen as a sign that the critique of capitalism, after being relegated to the margins for the previous thirty years, is making a comeback. Inviting Piketty to grace the Nelson Mandela stage, here at the heart of the South African academic establishment, feels like something of a coup. Perhaps more space is at last opening up to look at the real drivers of poverty and inequality in South Africa.

But things have already started going wrong. A couple of days ago, news came that Piketty's travel documents had not been in order. The man did not have enough blank pages in the back of his passport, and had been refused the right to enter South Africa by our doughty Home Affairs administration. Plan B, therefore, is that his lecture will be delivered via Skype, with a panel discussion to follow. Not ideal, and many people, deprived of the chance to see an academic star in person, have stayed away, but I have come anyway, hoping for an interesting discussion.

Then, right at the start of the event, this happens: seventeen students file unexpectedly into the hall, bearing banners that indicate that they represent Rhodes Must Fall and the UCT Left Students Forum, and that they are protesting against unjust labour policies at UCT. One of the banners ("UCT—we pay below the poverty line") bears a helpful footnote with the URL of a groundup.org.za article. The students mount the stage, where the assembled dignitaries are already waiting—including ex-Finance Minister Trevor Manuel and Njabulo Ndebele, an erstwhile Vice-Chancellor. There is a pregnant pause. Everyone waits to see what will happen next. The students burst into song—a mournfully delivered version of "Thina Sizwe". After which they remain standing, mutely facing the audience (and, for the moment, the live-streaming cameras), for a few minutes more. Eventually Ndebele rises and comes to the podium to welcome the audience and to announce a national initiative led by the Nelson Mandela foundation. The students silently file offstage. This unexpected interruption over, the event resumes as planned.

Except it doesn't. The Skype screen comes on and for a while we stare at the po-faced visage of the famous French professor, who is apparently unaware that he is live. After a while, the audience starts tittering. The screen goes dark again, and Trevor Manuel, who is MC for this event, explains that there appears to be a technical problem. Plan B—that there would be a Skype lecture by Prof Piketty, followed by a panel discussion—will now make way for Plan C, in which the panel discussion comes first, followed by the lecture.

Things get worse from there. Halfway through the presentation of the first panellist, Prof Olajide Oleyede from UWC's department of Anthropology, Piketty's visage appears again on the screen behind him. Oleyede, who is making a convoluted argument about the absence of sociology from Piketty's book, continues, apparently unaware of the image behind him. Piketty is looking increasingly grumpy, scowling and gesticulating expressively in a very Gallic way. Giggles ripple through the auditorium. After a while the live feed disappears again.

The next panellist is UCT's Prof Debbie Collier, whose talk focuses on the failure of labour market regulation in South Africa and how this had contributed to the murder of the 34 mine workers at Marikana. She warns about the deepening levels of inequality in South Africa, and how these are a direct consequence of the ways in which our labour markets work and the industrial relations system we have created. A good intervention, I think, pointing squarely to some of the most intractable problems at the heart of post-Apartheid society.

At this point the students return, singing and toyi-toying, and retake the stage. Collier smiles sweetly and retires instantly. For a while we listen to the singing. Then Manuel, who is after all an old Struggle activist, comes to the podium and tries to engage the students, addressing them in isiXhosa. They pay him not the slightest bit of attention. After a few more minutes the diminutive and rumpled figure of UCT Vice-Chancellor Max Price quietly hops on stage, makes a beeline for one of the students in the middle of the toyi-toying group, and starts chatting with him amiably. This produces some discussion in their ranks. A few students leave the singing and go into a huddle with Manuel and Price. After a while Manuel says that they will permit a statement of three minutes.

A female student (invisible in the group, but with a microphone) starts speaking. She tells us that she is probably not good at speaking and will mispronounce the words. This is because she is Black and female and excluded. (Her English sounds perfectly fine to me.) She then makes a short speech questioning labour outsourcing at UCT. There is both angry heckling and support from the audience. She says they object to the fact that we, here—Thomas Piketty and the Nelson Mandela Foundation—are "celebrating inequality" while workers are suffering outside, and that the people who should be here are excluded.

That's it. Trevor Manuel thanks them politely.

They file off stage.

After this, the event is basically over. The remaining panellists soldier bravely on, and UCT's Murray Leibrandt gamely takes the audience through Piketty's slides, but the energy has left the room. I have a leaden feeling in my stomach. Suddenly it feels as if this is not a gathering of "prominent people, debating significant social issues", but a pointless talk shop. The real action is outside. Manuel, I think to myself, missed a trick. Why not invite the students to stay and join the debate? Surely their energy should have been welcomed? Should they not be taken seriously—and challenged?

And what about the students? Why were they satisfied just to read a statement and leave? Instead of a debate, we've just had a Statement. Two different worlds: academic policy deliberation on the one side, polite and self-involved; on the other, activist anger, confrontational and declamatory.

What I remember today, looking back at that event, is how polite it all was, how restrained.

Divisions

TWO WEEKS LATER STUDENTS AT the University of the Witwatersrand protested against recently announced hikes in student fees. The protest spread swiftly and became a nationwide student uprising against the injustice of financial exclusions and crippling student debt. Within days the students' cause had broadened from the fee increases to include their deeper sense of cultural exclusion and the persistence of omnipresent white supremacy in academic institutions, still in place two decades after the transition to democracy. Their criticisms were sweeping, their rhetoric fiery; and their furious clarity brought into focus the harsh reality—so evident, yet so often ignored—of the betrayal of the promise of the dismantling of the racialised inequality bequeathed by Apartheid.

Like many of my colleagues, I was inspired and moved by their passion and their optimism. When the students occupied the Student Union building, my colleagues and I brought food and supplies for them. And when the #FeeswillFall movement at UWC called for the closure of campus a few days later, I was part of a small group of academics nominated by progressive members of staff to support the students and to attempt to mediate the growing rift between their leadership and the university management. For a couple of intense, somewhat scary but also exhilarating weeks I found myself playing a part in shuttle diplomacy between the students and the Vice-Chancellor's office, moving between the admin building and the university gates where the air was at times thick with rubber bullets and stinging clouds of teargas.

We came within reach of success, almost managing to get the student leaders to agree to a meeting mediated by the university Chancellor, Archbishop Thabo Makgoba. But that moment of rapprochement failed. As our group of "concerned academics" quickly learned, the initial, broadly based upwelling of student protest, in which we had seen the Student Union building next to our offices filled with students united in anger and a shared sense of challenge, had splintered within days into competing groups, mostly divided along political party lines. While the university executive had agreed to meet with the (broadly ANC aligned) Students' Representative Council, the legitimacy of these negotiations was disputed by students aligned with PASMA, who now pronounced themselves the true and authentic leaders of the uprising, and many of whom were bent on violent confrontation. The SRC, finding itself marginalised and outflanked, regarded any acknowledgement of their political rivals by the university authorities as a denial of their legitimacy as representatives of the student body. The university management, which was at that stage still quite inexperienced, (the Vice-Chancellor and his deputies had only recently been appointed) found itself caught in the middle.

I recall being on campus on the afternoon of Friday, 28 October 2015. The balmy spring weather of the previous week had given way to oppressive heat. Campus had been shut down. What remained of our "task team" of "concerned academics" (we had disbanded formally a few days earlier, lacking any real mandate) had just met with a rather depressed and gloomy Vice-Chancellor in his offices in the abandoned administration building. It had been agreed that the best way forward was to propose a meeting, not between the executive team and the protesting students, but between all the parties and the university management, mediated by the university's Chancellor, Archbishop Makgoba. We were crossing towards the student residences where protesting students were engaged in fierce confrontation, just outside the university gates, with the South African police. The police had not been allowed to come onto campus, but had (on their account) been responding to alleged incidents of stone throwing on Symphony Way. We headed towards Kovacs Student Village and Ruth First Residence, following the sounds of strife and the reek of teargas.

From those chaotic minutes my main memories are of the very different attitudes of the groups of students with whom we engaged. First, there were the students—mostly young women—who were the political officers of some of the formal student organisations that we had been talking to. While some of them had previously been inciting violence, they now agreed to mediation. But they also seemed marginalised and ignored. As far as I could make out, they were not even trying to get any traction. They hung back from the confrontation, looking spooked and scared.

Second, there were the young male students who had during the course of the day been involved in angry confrontations with police. We met a small number of them in the lee of Ruth First Residence. They were in a state of deep emotional trauma, in the grip of what seemed to be almost unbearable frustration and rage. I felt the presence of grief and hurt under their anger. I felt my heart go out to them. After a while we were able to enter into a space where speech was possible. We tried to convey the nature of the Vice-Chancellor's offer to them, but it was clear that this was not an offer they could respond to. The time for negotiation has passed! they shouted at us. They wanted immediate capitulation to their demands.

Third, there was a smaller group of much more level-headed young men. They had also been in the thick of the confrontation with the police but seemed actively involved in shaping the energy and direction of their fellow students. We spoke to one or two of them. While they were clearly tense and anxious, they seemed interested in responding strategically to the situation. When we told them that the Archbishop was willing to come to campus and that this presented a strategic possibility for a breakthrough, they seemed immediately to grasp that they would be able to claim the arrival of the Archbishop as their victory and announce it as such to their followers. They agreed that they would engage with their fellow students and lead them to the Student Centre to meet with the authorities.

But within minutes, the mobile confrontation between the students and the police had moved to a different part of campus. The confrontation outside Kovacs and Ruth First moved elsewhere. The entire situation dissolved. The moment had passed.

Fourth, what really alarmed me was that some people around me seemed to be calmly preparing for violence. At one point, while I was talking to one of the leadership figures (he was explaining to me that they were not interested in speaking with the Vice-Chancellor, who was merely a member of the capitalist management class protecting the profits of the University) a group of burly young men right next to us were not marching, not singing political songs, not shouting, not talking, but cheerfully and quite methodically preparing for violence, using crowbars and pick-axes to pry up large concrete kerbstones and then breaking them up into smaller, more throwable pieces. While I was not in any danger at that moment, I thought that the situation could become very unpredictable very soon. I did not want my skull to get into the path of either the police's rubber bullets or one of those kerbstones.

A few moments later I received a message from UWC management indicating that in view of the ongoing violence, the opportunity for negotiation had passed. My colleagues and I agreed that we had failed and beat a rueful retreat.

Within days events had spiralled out of control. From a (mostly) peaceful confrontation between students and the university management around issues that seemed, at least in principle, amenable to negotiation, the argument spiralled into open, unbridgeable and violent conflict. Campus slid into chaos. Students were shot with rubber bullets and beaten up. The campus medic was brutally assaulted by some of the very students who were in his care. Twitter and WhatsApp feeds were alive with rumours, some true but many false. The university community swiftly divided into two furiously opposed factions: those who saw the students as anarchic, unreasonable, and simply destructive, and those who took the students' side, blaming police and the university management for the deteriorating situation.

And I could not support either side. In the course of those few days my initial admiration for the striking students had been somewhat tempered. While I agreed with the justice of their cause and sympathised with their radical ambitions, their actual demand—for free tertiary education—seemed far from revolutionary to me; a middle-class project, not a pro-poor, egalitarian one. Their strategy and tactics, which took as their primary adversary the beleaguered and fragile university management rather than the government's ruinous tertiary education policies, seemed misguided. And I had growing reservations about their political vocabulary and practice, which was articulated in the language of confrontation, domination, coercion and political command.

It was a confusing, unsettling time.

So I wrote. I sat down at my laptop and wrote a long, thoughtful, discursive piece. As I had learned to do, I thought aloud, letting the words slide onto the page. I argued that there were a number of overly simplistic narratives going around about the nature of what was happening on our campus—narratives offering little reliable grip on the complexities of the actual situation. There was a real risk that progressive academics, identifying too uncritically with the narratives that a relatively small group of students were putting about, were misreading the situation and losing their ability to intervene effectively in the shrinking space that remained. Even more worryingly, I warned, there was a danger that the rapidly solidifying readings that were developing on different sides of the conflict could lead to a situation where progressive academics concerned about the future of a liberatory academic project at UWC would find themselves marginalised, at odds with the rest of the campus community and alienated from the executive.

As the sentences unspooled, it became possible for me to see a third place to stand, a position not captured by the passionate narratives of the moment, a position that recognised the complexity and ambiguity of the moment. It offered no easy answers, but it did suggest ways of engaging that would not actively make things worse. I still felt, like many of my colleagues, that there was something precious and beautiful in our students' earnest and radical passion. But we had to find a different way of engaging with it: not by taking sides, but by making connections.

I was heartened by the response to my intervention. I received emails from other progressive academics at UWC who felt I had given voice to reservations in their own heads, and who commended me for trying to articulate a space from which polarisation could be ameliorated, not exacerbated. The Vice-Chancellor wrote to me warmly, commending me for my intervention. Most heartening of all was the support of my sister Marijke, recently arrived from UKZN but already much more plugged into the networks of campus life than I was—and more able than me, also, to penetrate the overheated texture of the current debate with her warm and grounded common sense.

Sitting next to Marijke at a tumultuous town hall meeting called by our Vice-Chancellor, I had felt the warm glow of pride. My attempt to help mediate the conflict had not worked, but words and reason could perhaps still help cool things down.

And then this happened: my colleague Ben Cousins, who had been director of our Institute before I took over and who was therefore a mentor to me and something of an elder statesman to all of us at PLAAS, took the microphone. Dapper and confident in his black corduroy jacket, he seemed the picture of the charismatic senior academic. And to my dismay he proceeded to lambaste the university executive, hauling them over the coals for their intransigence and their supposed refusal to meet with the students. I was horrified and taken aback because Ben's version of events—that a paranoid and authoritarian university executive was refusing to engage with students who just wanted to be heard—was entirely out of touch with the facts. I was aghast, too, at the spectacle of Ben, a confident, white "radical" academic, berating the black leadership of a black-led institution. Perhaps he thought he was speaking up for African students against a "coloured" executive he perceived as conservative. But whatever his intention, it came across (at least to me!) as the epitome of unconscious white arrogance. This could hardly bode well for the relationship between our Institute and the university on whose goodwill we depended.

Ben followed this intervention up by circulating a think piece of his own in which he took me to task for what he said was my misreading of the situation. What shocked me about his piece was not so much the public broadside, but the way in which he did it, unkindly misrepresenting my position, quoting me out of context, mounting an attack that seemed to me hostile and unfair.

The wind was taken out of my sails. I felt betrayed. Even more unnerving was the fact that my senior colleagues backed Ben and coldly informed me of their dismay at my actions. My attempts to intercede in a rapidly polarising situation, to create spaces for dialogue, to defend the fraying fabric of our campus community, it seemed, were not welcome. There was no space for complexity. It was the students versus the university management, and we had to choose a side.

The conflict was no longer just on campus. It was inside our Institute. Some of my colleagues, particularly support staff, I could see were severely discomfited at the division opening up within our close-knit intellectual family. Office meetings became stilted and uncomfortable. Ben and I continued to debate unproductively, speaking past each other.

In the end, seeking to keep the peace and prevent disagreement from splitting our little Institute, I backed down. I stopped writing. I met with Ben outside the School of Public Health, where he had been teaching, and offered to bury the hatchet. We shook hands awkwardly, Ben offering his left hand and giving a twisted grin. I wandered back to my car across the abandoned campus. The glass doors of B-Block had been shattered. Rubbish was lying everywhere. A small group of students—AZASM if I recall correctly—were chanting Africanist slogans. Their voices were angry and bitter, and they looked at me with palpable hostility. I felt alone and troubled. Did I even belong here?

And that's how 2015 ended for me: with a feeling of unease and alienation. A rift had opened up between my close colleagues and me. I had believed that I was part of a group that was committed to the value of critical thought, of non-partisan sense making.

But in these new, more polarised times, it seemed the rules had changed. You chose your side. You aligned.

I did not want to end up being isolated.

So I shut my mouth.

Part 5

Finding words

THIS HAS BEEN A MEANDERING story. But I am trying to understand what was going on for me, around me, when I blundered into the confrontation on that February morning. I had been moved by Vuyokazi's discomfiture, but I had not spoken angrily, I had not been indignant. Barnor's question, *wilt thou then disown me?*, had certainly been in my mind: I had been aware that this was not something that I could just let go. But I had not wanted to confront the man at the oak table. I had quite deliberately avoided directly accusing him of racism, not because I wanted to soft-soap him but because I knew it would not be useful. I wanted to make him stop and think, to admonish him, to draw his attention to the nature of his actions. Not that I had been particularly successful.

So, what now? I was still unsettled and unnerved. But I was also angry. Or I felt I was entitled to be. I had been insulted and threatened for doing the right thing, for standing up (or trying to stand up) for the dignity of another person. And to make it worse, Virgin Active management seemed to be perfectly fine with that. A man had spat in my face and had threatened to kill me, but, on the other hand, Justus and Labuschagne had pointed out, I had made the man feel I was calling him a racist.

Really?

So I wrote it all up. I had a blog, remember? I fired it up again, and I recounted the whole traumatic scene as it had unfolded, sparing no detail. And I tried to say what was at stake, tried to sort out my jumbled thoughts and feelings.

I found myself saying that I was actually not interested in naming and shaming the men who had confronted me. Other than the issue of their threats of future violence, I did not have a beef with them. I did not wish any recompense. I did not want an apology. Rather, this was a matter between me and the club. What did *they* stand for? While I had not suffered physical harm, I had been subjected to repeated verbal and physical abuse in public; a humiliating and unpleasant experience. It should not have happened, and I should not have to worry about it happening again.

Most importantly, I wanted the club to back me up on this. Not only was the behaviour of the men completely unacceptable; it was also against their own rules, which expressly, in plain language, prohibited not only verbal and physical abuse, but also forbade the taking of photographs of other members of the club. Were they willing to stand by their rules (and by me), or not?

Here, I thought, lay the crux of the whole matter, the reason it mattered at all:

The whole experience is, for me, worth thinking and writing up because, in a small way, it casts a brief and sobering light on some of the dynamics of racial privilege, power, and violence in South Africa.

The point for me is not simply the casual racism that I witnessed, in which an entitled, middle class white man vented his irritation by belittling and mocking an African woman who never did him any harm. That, as we all know, happens every day.

Rather, it is the almost psychotic response my challenge provoked—and the gym management's bland, hedging protection of the men.

Challenging racist behaviour is not, apparently, something that merits a rational civilised response. Rather, it is a threat, an insult, and has to be shut down as such. What the incident seems to tell me—a dispiriting and depressing thought it is—is that in our society, calling a white man a racist is a violation of civility. It's a provocation.

And the venom and rage it calls forth …?
Well, I guess I was just asking for it.
Or that's what the club appears to think.

A shock

THIS WAS ON FRIDAY, 19 February, exactly two weeks after my memorable breakfast encounter.

I felt relieved and pleased with myself. Part of it was just the satisfaction of being able to find words for what had happened, for what had been bothering me. I must admit that in part I just enjoyed sticking it to Virgin Active, calling them to account, and—yes!—naming and shaming them for their shoddy behaviour. And although I did not want to acknowledge it to myself at the time, I also enjoyed being able to make myself part of a vindicatory narrative. I was not like those other whites! I stood up against racism! I had done the right thing!

My blog piece was a success. It was far and away the most popular piece of writing I have ever done. These, you must remember, were the early days of Black Twitter. Within minutes of publication, my piece was being re-posted and re-shared. It went viral. Within an hour, it had been read and shared tens of thousands of times. My email inbox filled up with messages from people sharing their own experiences of racism or of witnessing it. Within two hours, I was contacted by Ross Faragher-Thomas, CEO of Virgin Active, who wanted to share with me his distress at the unfortunate experiences I had been subjected to, and promising to make good.

And then this happened: late on that same day I received a Facebook post from the friend of a friend, a man called Shaun Shelley. Shelly was a researcher who worked in the field of drug addiction and harm reduction, a man who had some understanding, therefore, of the workings of Cape Town's criminal underworld. He wrote that he was not surprised at the club management's response. Judging from my description, the men in question might well be people who worked for the protection rackets extorting money from Cape Town's nightclubs and restaurants. They could quite possibly be associates of a man called M_____. If that were the case, Virgin Active's reluctance to prosecute the men might be due not to complicity with the structures of white supremacy, but to fear. They might be worried about reprisals.

I had never heard of M_____ .

I Googled him.

My screen filled up with hits.

M_____, it turned out, was one of those people that Cape Town's newspapers like to describe as a "controversial businessman", meaning someone self-evidently criminal but with access to lawyers.

I did an image search.

In the canon of modern psychological thought, it is William James who is credited with first proposing the idea that knowledge arrives via your body. Fear and the awareness of danger do not arrive first in the mind, in the form of a rational apprehension. Before you even know that you know, you feel the leaden sensation in your gut, the dull feeling of energy leaking out of your body, the cold shimmer of adrenalin.

I did not want this to be happening. There was M_____, clean-cut and confident, striding ebulliently out of a Cape Town courthouse, triumphant after beating 313 counts of running an extortion racket. And there, right next to him, chubbier than in real life but definitely the same person, was the second man, the man who had spat in my face and threatened to kill me. His name was A_____. He was M_____'s fixer, his muscle.

My skin prickling, I read on. There were many stories about A_____, who was heavily implicated in accusations of running protection rackets and who featured in numerous stories of violence, the most alarming of which was an account of a dramatic shootout, a bar fight that had spilled out into the street the year before. More than 50 gunshots had been fired in the parking lot outside a Bellville nightclub. Both A_____ and his adversary had been wounded; A_____ had been shot in the leg. (I recalled his lurching walk, his limp as he lumbered around the table to spit at me.) Now at last I understood his references to the fact that he had "black friends", and Justus's statement that he was part of an organisation that "employed lots of black people". Well, that was one way of putting it! Justus had been referring to the fact that A_____ was allied with a notorious Cape Flats gangster. When he had been inviting me to Google him and had bragged that he was one of Cape Town's biggest criminals, he was not merely boasting. He was pretty much telling it like it was.

All my colleagues had left. The office was empty. There was no one to talk to. I tried to collect my scattered thoughts. Everything had changed. Suddenly A_____'s threats, his promise to slit my throat, his colleague's statement that they would track me down, and above all that photograph, took on a new meaning. I had to think about my safety. Asking Virgin Active to expel them would be very much the wrong thing to do. My desire for vindication suddenly seemed stupid and foolish. My best course of action seemed to be to find a way of letting the matter drop before things escalated further.

I took down my blog. Not because I feared that A_____ and his friend would read it, but given the public pressure on the club to act, it could only complicate matters. I also realised that I did not want to expose Vuyokazi to any further attention.

Other, much more uncomfortable thoughts occurred. John Justus and Virgin Active Management had clearly known exactly who I had been dealing with. Could they not have warned me? Why had they not dissuaded me from further confrontation?

I called Isak Labuschagne, regional manager of Virgin Active. I told him I had new information. We needed to meet, and urgently. Not at The Point. He agreed to meet me at Wembley Square, where I went to swim every day.

We met the next morning. I ordered a flat white. Labuschagne sat across from me, politely and watchfully, with folded hands. I had come across new information, I told him. I had found out the identity of the men who had threatened me. I knew who they were. Was he aware, I asked him, of who and what they were, of what kind of men we were dealing with? No, he had no idea, Labuschagne assured me, no idea at all. I opened my iPad. My hands were shaking with rage. I showed him the picture of A_____ with M_____. It was this man, I said. A well-known thug and gangster. Could he confirm it? Without missing a beat, Labuschagne affirmed, yes, that was him, they knew all about him.

There were many instructive moments for me during the course of this story, but I must tell you this was one of the most unpleasant: the recognition that this unctuous man sitting opposite me, polite and friendly and tidy and concerned, was not to be trusted. That despite all his protestations, he did not have my back; that he would say one thing one moment, and another thing the next, without batting an eyelid, depending only on what corporate loyalty dictated. It was at this moment, I think, that I really knew I was not safe; that everything, *everything*, was about minimising risk to company.

Labuschagne said he hoped I understood the difficult position they had been in. They would really have liked to act against the men, he said, but they lacked evidence. They had, he assured me, a no tolerance attitude towards racism. Zero tolerance! Zero! But they had spoken to the cashier, and she had told them that there had not been a problem. She had not felt they had been racist at all. There had been no CCTV footage. Their hands had been tied.

I swallowed my rage and told him that I was dropping my case. I was no longer asking Virgin Active to expel A_____ and his friend. Doing so would not help; in fact, it would probably make things more dangerous. For the same reason, I said, I had also taken down my blog post. Labuschagne was visibly relieved at this and told me sympathetically that he completely understood my concerns. He complimented me on my moral integrity. (It takes one to know one, I guess.) He promised that they would not do anything that would allow A____ and his friend to identify me. He reiterated that he wished me to understand that Virgin Active was deeply opposed to racism in all its shapes and forms, and that he hoped I now understood why they had not expelled these men.

I contacted Sea Point Police Station, an institution that I now understood were quite probably in the pocket of A_____ and M_____, and told them I was dropping the case.

I met with Phila Zulu, head of legal at Virgin Active. He assured me that A_____ and M_____ only ever came to The Point, not to Wembley Square, where I usually worked out. I had no reason to fear that I would encounter them there. We agreed that in that case, there was no reason for the club to bar them anymore. We also agreed that there would be little point in the club trying to facilitate a meeting with the men or trying to facilitate a reconciliation. It was best just to leave matters be.

Keeping safe

WHAT NOW? I WAS IN unknown territory. I did not know how to make sense of my situation. Was I in danger? Was I not? And what could I do about it?

Part of the problem was that the whole affair did not make sense even by the standards of the criminal underworld. As Shaun Shelly explained to me, A_____ and M_____ were at that time under intensive investigation by Cape Town's anti-gang unit. Announcing to a complete stranger that he was the biggest fucking criminal in Cape Town was not really a wise thing to do. Had A_____ just been having a bad morning? Was it just a momentary flash of rage? Or was it something more serious?

Pearlie Joubert, a friend from those early days in the Stellenbosch counterculture and now a veteran of investigative reporting—it was she who had blown the whistle on the *Sunday Times*'s smear campaign on the SARS "rogue unit"—told me that she had suspected from the beginning that it had been A_____. A small-time thug, she said, who clung to M_____'s apron strings; a bully who got off on hurting street children and those weaker than him. Usually I would not have to worry about such a person; in the normal run of things, a white university professor would be *bo sy vuurmaakplek*, above his pay grade.

The thing about A_____'s way of dealing with people, she warned, was its brutality. People like him were fundamentally insecure, deeply threatened. All that mattered to them was whether you would physically challenge them, whether you would humiliate them just as they sought to humiliate you. If he detected a hint of weakness, he would strike, she told me, instinctively, like an animal.

This was a new thought to me. Had I responded differently, had I gotten in A_____'s face and told him to fuck off, things might have turned out differently. By being mild, by not pushing back, I had signalled to him that he could push me around with impunity.

She had also a word of advice. A_____ and his ilk, she said, disliked publicity. They loved acting in the shadows. Don't let him think you are afraid! Expose him, she said. Make it public! This made a kind of sense. And it would give me a sense of agency, a sense of control. But it was a high-risk game. I couldn't quite see myself getting into parking lot shootouts with this man. And I did not only have myself to think about: there was also Jay and her daughters. If things escalated, I would be putting them in danger as well.

At the very least I had to think quite practically about what to make of A_____ and his friend's threats. The remark about knowing I drove a Toyota might just have been intended to frighten me, but I had to take it seriously. Could they somehow have planted a tracking device in my car? I took the car to an auto-electrician reputed to know about such technology; he said there was nothing. More seriously, Pearlie had pointed out that, as someone with friends within the police, it would be child's play for A_____ to find out who I was and where I lived: what could I do about that? Vary your habits, most of the people I asked suggested: don't always drive the same route home. Advice straight from a spy thriller, but hard to actually implement. Try varying your routines if you are a house-husband and a university professor. There are only so many pathways to your lock-up garage. At any rate, I decided to keep my head down. Wait it out. Hopefully it would all blow over.

"Naming and shaming"

MEANWHILE THERE WAS THAT BLOG. I had taken it down, but it had been widely shared, and was causing ripples of its own. People wrote to me to ask why it had disappeared. Why was Virgin Active not doing something? Could they help? Put pressure on the club to identify the men, to "name and shame" them? Well-intentioned messages no doubt, but not helpful in these particular circumstances. I put up a bland notice on my blog, saying that Virgin Active was being terrifically helpful, and politely deflected the offers of help.

But still. I had taken it upon myself to write about the whole thing in the first place. Now I was invested. Taking it down rankled, to tell the truth. I had allowed myself, once again, to be silenced, to have my mouth shut. I did not want to let go of my "piece". I wanted to make sense of it, to grasp it in words, to understand it, to craft a story around it.

Most of all, I did not want to be intimidated. As I reflected on it, the strange thing about the contretemps with A_____ was that it was not a new experience. It brought back many memories. In my boyhood in Stellenbosch, I'd been a pupil at Paul Roos Gymnasium, an institution where, at least in the 1970s and 1980s, bullying and thuggery (on the part of both students and teachers) had been part of institutional culture.

One of the oddest things about the whole experience, indeed, had been how familiar it felt. I'd been there before. Thinking back on it now, it seemed to me that one of the most important lessons I had learned about dealing with bullies was that if you allow yourself to be shaken too much by vague threats of reprisal, the bully has won. The bully's contract with you is: Agree with me that civil behaviour is a sham. Agree with me that the only reality is this hold I have over you, my humiliating encounter with you behind the cafeteria wall when no one was watching. Agree with me that you are worth nothing. The threat to you never happened. Be silent. Live quietly in fear.

Or I will come for you.

So I sat down to redraft my blog piece to try to make sense of what had happened. I still thought that the point of the whole story was not simply the casual racism that I had witnessed but the almost psychotic response my challenge had evoked.

In this respect, A_____ and his friend's criminal backgrounds were not really a central part of the story. True: he had been able to call on and use a trained and feral aggressiveness that's not at the disposal of many of the rest of us. But in other ways it had not been all that unusual. In an eerie parallel to my own experience, only a few days later, journalist Lisa Golden had had a similar experience in a Johannesburg parking lot, although her interlocutor was a thirty year old woman with blonde highlights and an iPad—the kind of person who a few years later would be called a Karen—instead of a man with a history of nightclub parking lot shootouts. Reflecting on the torrent of abuse she experienced in response to her mild remonstrations, Golden said:

> … *yesterday, the level of violence and hatred and venom spat at me from a complete stranger for confronting her lack of manners, her lack of humanity, her lack of respect, showed me as a white person how desperately far behind we are as a community. How deeply entrenched in our privilege. How disconnected we can be from a country and economy that's purpose for so long has been to serve us. Coddle us. Pander to our tantrums.*
>
> … *if you are out there, and you are reading this, please act. I don't know if what I did was going about things the wrong way. But I've ripped off the plaster. You and I both know you see a conversation like that at least once a week. It's time we hold our own community to account.*

So far so good. But I felt it necessary to probe further. *Why* would even a gentle challenge provoke such a violent and defensive reaction? Unacceptable as A_____ and Golden's adversary's reactions were, I felt I needed to make sense of them. Where did they come from? What was at stake?

It would be easy to simply say, well, that's white racists for you: they are a savage, horrible bunch. This is just the way they behave. That would be a comforting story.

But perhaps we should probe further. What was going on here? Why would accusations of racism provoke such savage responses in the first place? What exactly actually had happened there, at 9.30 in the morning in the sunlit space of Kauai at The Point Virgin Active? What could I learn, both with my brain and my body?

Brain first: it seemed to me that at the heart of my and A_____'s confrontation was an intense and charged set of transactions around identity, status, respect and fear. As white men with power and money, his friend's routine disrespect of a black waitress and cashier was a small daily ritual, affirming his rank and personal supremacy. As a white man in a pinstripe shirt, obviously coming from a much more comfortable background, sitting smugly behind my MacBook Pro, speaking to them in poncy Afrikaans, I had not only been bringing awareness to the unacceptable dimensions of their behaviour: I had also been pulling rank. I had been chastising them. I had been telling them, in effect, that *this is no way for a white man to behave*. And I did so by deploying one of the most potent, shaming accusations available in our society today, saying in effect: you are not one of us.

And this brought me to body learning. What I remembered about the confrontation was not so much fear as *shame*. Thinking back to the incident, remembering what it was like to be there, what it feels like when someone spits in your face in public and no one does anything about it, it now seemed to me that the core of what had happened was the ritual enactment of *humiliation*.

A few days after I had learned about the possible identity of my adversaries, someone had sent me an article on violence in Britain's high security prisons. It argued that male rage and the threat of violence were all about responding to, and inflicting powerful feelings of shame and humiliation. This, I now reflected, had been what was going on with the bullies at Paul Roos. They had always been the slightly lower-status kids. The kids who were not doing so well academically, who came from poorer backgrounds, sometimes even from backgrounds that were whispered to be not quite white enough; or just kids from unloving, messed-up homes. Kids who were constantly told they were "less than", and who found temporary relief in brutality and cruelty towards those weaker than them.

There was clearly a big difference between schoolyard bullies (who often do their persecutory thing in secret) and adult gangsters asserting their status with threats of violence. But still the two worlds felt connected. When I "called" the men on their actions, I had been putting them in their place—and they had responded viciously in kind.

A memory came suddenly to me. It had been earlier that year, perhaps a week or two before the Virgin Active incident. I'd been queuing for coffee at the deli at the Gardens Centre. This was usually a frustrating experience; the counter was for some reason almost always understaffed, with one harried black *barista* having to run back and forth taking orders, handling payments and making coffee. The white woman in the queue before me had behaved abominably, gracelessly insulting the *barista* for her slow service. On that occasion, I now remembered, I had not confronted the white woman. Instead, when my turn arrived, I indicated to the staffer that she could take her time. I apologised for the rudeness of the woman before me. How do you manage to stay so patient, I had asked her, when people behave like that? The woman had simply smiled warmly and shrugged.

I had forgotten this brief encounter. But now it seemed to me that this approach might have been much more helpful than my rather clumsy attempt to school the nightclub gangster. Certainly Vuyokazi had not benefited at all; in fact, she'd later probably felt that the scene I had made had got her into trouble.

All in all, the whole thing had made me think again about the calls that were circulating about the need to "take a stand", to signal one's disapproval of racist behaviour, to say #racismstopswithme. This politics of performance, this requirement to demonstrate "where one stood", it now seemed to me, was part of the problem. In fact, for the previous 20 years or so, this is how liberal white South Africans had mostly dealt with the historical reality of racism. We disavowed it. We had treated it as a sin, as something to be expunged and spat out, or a crime ("hate speech") that had to be punished and silenced. We had created a new, unspoken social contract, in which to be found guilty of racism was to be cast out of the body politic; to have no right to speak or to be part of our new democracy. We had created a culture in which racism was always something *someone else* did: those terrible whites over there, with whom we will have nothing to do, *want ons is nie so nie* (we are not like that).

When I had first published my blog piece the most common response from readers had been that the men needed to be exposed: to be *named and shamed*.

But shaming someone was not helpful. It was denial and repression of what was there. It was scapegoating. It was rejection. Most of all, it would not solve the problem. It only served to drive the reality of racism underground, unacknowledged but still real. Shaming, I now found myself thinking, is something *one* person does to *another*. Unlike guilt, which involves an examination of self and of debts unpaid, shaming is something that I do to someone else so that I can feel good about myself.

What is the alternative? Was I saying now that the behaviour of those men must be understood? Yes, I was. Was I saying it should therefore be excused? Obviously not.

But I thought we needed to find a way of moving our talk about racism from the register of sin and shame, something that is to be expunged and denied, to the register of accountability; something to be acknowledged and owned.

I wrote in my blog:

So what I will say is this, and especially to my white South African compatriots. Do not react to the behaviour of those

> two men by pointing fingers. Avoid that cheap superiority.
> Moral outrage is the easy option here. But it disavows a
> deeper, underlying truth. We are all part of this problem. We
> are all part of this dynamic of shame and rage. None of us are
> free of it.

By this time two more weeks had passed. I felt considerably lighter in heart and mind. Nothing bad had happened. And I was pleased with my writing. I'd managed to turn the horrible and chaotic welter of feelings into which I had been plunged into something else: into understanding, into compassion, into a way of making sense of what had happened.

I circulated it to many of my friends, all of whom responded with appreciation and with advice about how it could be improved.

But could I publish it?

Perhaps not just then. From what I knew of him, it was highly unlikely that A_____ or his friend were up at night reading anti-racist blogs. But at the same time, it seemed wise not to tempt fate. When readers of my blog wrote in to ask for updates, I responded vaguely and evasively. When the dust settled, I promised myself, I would put the blog up again. Eventually. "The only thing I can do about this man's threats", I wrote in the final (unpublished) version of my blog, "is to pay them no mind."

Part 6

In the parking garage

How do you describe what it's like to be violently assaulted in broad daylight?

I am able, I think, to do a pretty good job of conveying the taste and feel and experience of a particular slice of more or less coherent, meaningful reality. But being punched in the face in a shopping mall parking lot by a total stranger with no warning is a different proposition entirely. It's not an experience you can easily describe, because a key part of the experience is that *reality itself* has suddenly been subject to a hole or glitch. All at once there's a jump cut. Something that you never contemplated happening has suddenly, with no warning, very much happened—and there you are. In the middle of it, on the ground of the parking garage, pain exploding in your nose, blood dripping on your clothes, your phone and keys scattered on the ground. You hear footsteps running away, and you realise belatedly that you've been wrong all along about what's been going on; you're not in the story you thought you were in, or you're not the one shaping this story anyway; a story in which, even as you were happily walking around, thinking your thoughts, someone had other plans for you. You've been punched in the face, and your assailant is already running away, and what the fuck has just happened?

It was Tuesday, 8 March 2016. It had already been a bleak, horrible morning. The previous day, Franziska Blöchliger, the teenage daughter of a family we knew, had been brutally raped and murdered while on a run in Tokai forest. This had happened in broad daylight. She had become separated from her mother, and a group of young men had overwhelmed her. The news had spread like wildfire through our social network, reaching us first through the Facebook posts and Instagram messages of Jay's teenage daughters. It was news that could not be comprehended, that I experienced mostly as a heavy numb sense of horror that sucked out all possibility of feeling or thought. I remember reading Twitter posts from young black people, voicing outrage at the media sensation around Franziska's death; it showed, they said, that in South Africa, white lives mattered while black lives did not. Franziska, in fact, had not been white, but I was too numb, too heavy with horror to correct them.

Violence and the threat of it was all around us. The Fallist movement was still in full swing, and so were the processes of polarisation that swirled around it. Only a few days before, students had burned down the science faculty of the University of the Northwest, another "historically black university" with no conceivable role today in the maintenance of white supremacy. Meanwhile, white students had assaulted black students protesting a rugby game at the University of the Free State, an institution whose Vice-Chancellor, Jonathan Jansen, had made a career of describing how they had solved the race problem there. More and more student leaders were openly calling for violence. A piece in the *Daily Maverick* had quoted a member of the Fees Must Fall movement at Wits opining that "Violence will bring an end to the world as we know it and cleanse all the evil, give rise to a completely new world where the only race that matters is the human race". I had been aghast at the arrogance and ignorance of such a statement. Richard Pithouse had written a thinkpiece commenting eloquently on the shortcomings of the naïve millennialism underlying this utterance, but his criticism seemed muted and fell short of confronting the ease with which South Africans seemed to be ready to excuse violence when an issue was aligned with their sympathies.

Monday evening had been a bad night. I sat up late with a heavy sense of disquiet and dread, watching and taking part in increasingly ill-tempered Twitter exchanges. I got into a war of words with Black First, Land First activist Lindsay Maasdorp, who had called for students to follow the leadership of the Northwest students and to "bring fire" to all South African campuses.

Lacking sleep, I missed going to gym that morning.

Missing gym, I decided to deviate from my normal route and to stop over at the Kloof Street Kauai to pick up a wrap for lunch.

Just a hair before nine I turned into the parking facility in the basement of the Lifestyle on Kloof shopping mall. My parking fairy was working: I parked in pole position, right next to the boom at the entrance, mere metres from the lobby. I remember I parked slightly askew, and wondered whether the owner of the red Ford in the next bay would take umbrage. Never mind, I would be quick, I would be gone before he returned. It was a quiet morning. I walked over the zebra crossing that leads to the entrance of the mall. I was dimly conscious of a burly and urbane black man exiting the mall, coming out as I went in, fixing me sharply in his gaze as he did so. Then there was the stunning impact of a blow to my face. I remember seeing my keys and wallet fly through the air. I remember uttering an undignified squawk of surprise. I remember feeling humiliated even at that moment. I fell heavily onto my back. Blood was spattering onto the cement. A man was running away—why? Another man was getting out of his car, rushing towards me with a handkerchief in his hand. Do people still carry handkerchiefs, I wondered? I was surrounded by people, all chattering in a panic and issuing contradictory commands. One woman—white, stylishly dressed, slender, imperious—instructed me in no uncertain terms to lie flat on my back right there in the parking lot and put my head completely back. This was clearly idiotic. I could feel blood pooling in my nose and collecting in my sinuses. If I were to lie down on my back, all of that stuff would be streaming into my throat. Not good. What to do? Well, I decided, in a situation where everyone is losing their heads, someone's got to take charge, and that person appeared to be me. I scrabbled around rather uncertainly and wobbled to my feet. I was conscious that my back was clearly injured. Not good at all. What had happened? Who was that man? Why had he hit me? Was it the owner of the red Ford? Was this Lindsay Maasdorp's doing? Somewhat to my surprise, I seemed able to stand, albeit uncertainly. Good. We were making progress. My back was really sore. The man with the handkerchief had somehow produced an absorbent green towel. Much better, although it, too, was rapidly getting soaked. Blood everywhere. A smart young black woman from centre management was there, briskly issuing commands. They wanted to get me to safety, to the hospital. (They wanted me out of public view, I thought. They did not want to scare the customers.) They said I should go to a doctor. What about the nurse in the pharmacy upstairs, I asked? They have a nurse there. Take me to her. She's good. Or get her down here. Someone ran off. I was escorted into the centre manager's office. The very efficient young woman was calling the police. I needed to call work, to tell them I would not be coming in. I needed to call Jay, to tell her what had happened. I needed to call Kauai: my smoothie and my wrap had been ordered already, and they would be wondering why I was not there to pick them up. I managed to find my phone and texted work, and Jay: *I've been assaulted*, I said. The text looked strange, melodramatic.

At some point the security guard appeared. He had enterprisingly and courageously chased after my assailant. He returned with some very pertinent observations. The gentleman who had hit me had been waiting for me, he said. He had clearly recognized me, and my car. (The security guard mimicked the man's sharp double take as he clocked me). He was not a South African gentleman, the security said. He was Congolese. He looked like a bouncer.

Then I knew.

I did not want it to be this, I thought. I wanted it to be something else. But it wasn't something else. I remembered A_____'s promise to send one of his black buddies to beat me up.

He had been as good as his word.

The CCTV camera above the mall entrance captured the whole thing very nicely. It shows a burly, well-built man entering at a jog trot, following me down the slope of the entrance ramp a few moments after my car passes through the boom. He stops and carefully notes where my car is and where I am parking. He disappears into the lobby of the mall. A few other customers pass, unmolested and unremarked. I come out of my car, shooting a worried look at my incompetent parking. Bouncer man comes striding out of the lobby, hauls off and punches me in one confident, practiced movement. I fall clumsily to the ground.

He lopes away.

It looks easy, comfortable, practiced; he probably did not even break a sweat. You could use it as a training video. How to pop a white man in the face.

A tidy little packet of violence: a message from the street.

Counting the cost

As packages go, it was a very economical one. One of the thoughts that repeatedly visited me afterwards is how easy it is for someone trained in violence to inflict damage on someone not expecting it. All you need to do is to emerge for a moment from the stream of strangers who pass by your target every day. Do your thing and disappear. No risk, really; you just need to know your stuff. And he could have done much more. He could have used a knife, a gun, his boots. As it was, it was a single blow to the eye. As professionally administered violence goes, it is probably the basic unit. Entry-level.

A quantum of violence.

As it was, it was bad enough. The security guard who had chased after my attacker said the man had been wearing black finger gloves. These sometimes have weighted knuckles. SAP gloves, they are called, as I learned in my subsequent explorations on the internet. That single punch to my face inflicted significant damage. An X-ray scan taken at the hospital later that morning showed that the man had broken my nose, fractured my cheekbone, and caused a blow-out fracture of the orbit of my left eye. Not bad, for one punch.

It could have been worse. Blowout fractures can lead to problems such as enophthalmos, in which the eye sinks back into the eye socket; not only unsightly but also leading to diplopia (double vision). Preventing this requires expensive and tricky reconstructive surgery. In my case, that was not judged necessary. The specialist I visited a few days later decided surgery would not be needed. The blowout was minimal and there was little danger that my optic muscles would be damaged or snagged.

Two days after the event, the doorbell rang at my home. A courier was waiting at the door, bearing a large and rather ugly bouquet of flowers. There was no message. Where had it come from? The courier shrugged and showed me the manifest.

Virgin Active headquarters in Claremont.

For a few weeks, whenever I used my phone to text *I have been*, the IOS autocorrect feature would helpfully suggest *assaulted*.

In time, the bruises faded. My nose is still pretty much the same shape as before. There is a slight, almost unnoticeable asymmetry to my face that was not there before. My orbital blowout fracture has also had some long-term consequences: my left eye is a couple of millimetres lower than the right, and I do in fact suffer from mild diplopia. Most of the time I do not notice it, but reading and writing is much more tiring than before. And when I look up at night, I see two moons in the sky, like that guy in Murakami's interminable novel *1Q84*.

The most troublesome physical injury was to my back, caused when I fell heavily against the kerbstone at the parking lot boom. No actual damage to my spine, but significant trauma to the muscles around it. I had chronic back pain for months after the incident. I struggled to lift heavy loads, and I could not lie down or sleep comfortably. For a while I visited an American body worker in Green Point who was able to release the locked muscle spasms that kept me in pain, but he turned out to be a Trump supporter, and started needling me about my liberal views. *During sessions,* mind you. I did not return. I found a yoga teacher who could help me, and learned a new language of the body, new skills of balance and strength that I had not known before.

What about safety?

After the incident, I was put in touch with General Jeremy Veary, stalwart head of Cape Town's anti-gang unit. One of his lieutenants, a man with the poetic name of Anthony Vertue, interviewed me. I met Vertue at Truth, a hipster coffee shop in the heart of A_____ and M_____'s territory. Vertue's theory was that had A_____ been alone at the time of our altercation, nothing would have happened. His colleague, the man I had admonished, had probably been an important associate, someone in front of whom he could not lose face. Hence his reaction. It was unlikely that anything more would happen. He could get A_____ arrested, he said, on the basis of my dockets, but that might jeopardise me. But he would see to it, he said, that a message would be sent to A_____ informing him that it would not be a good idea to give me any more trouble.

Another friend, whose brother was a nightclub owner and who dealt regularly with M_____'s extortion racket, enquired indirectly and carefully about the matter. Was the beef ongoing? Word came back that it was not; the matter was regarded as settled.

Healing nicely

June, Cape Town, same year, two in the morning. My friends and I are at a nightclub in the city centre. We have been to a post-Afrika Burn decompression party. The venue is filled with DJs and revellers reliving for a moment the memories and experiences of being together in Tankwa Town in the Karoo. I have taken a break from the oppressive heat and the overwhelming throb of the music and I'm outside, breathing the fresh air of this rainy night. The street is thronged with partygoers and waiting Ubers; the steps are sticky with something, probably spilled drinks. Although I am surrounded by people, I have for a moment become separated from my friends.

Then a large man comes up the stairs right in front of me. He has reddish, curly hair and a boyish face, but he is, as they say, built. He is dressed in the black garb and heavy combat boots of the outfit who are providing security at the club. He peers into my face with concern. You're doing well, he says in a friendly tone. Your face is healing nicely. Then he turns away and melts into the night.

A similar thing happens three months later, at my health club at Wembley Square. Reassured by club management's assurances that A_____ and his friends only ever go to Virgin Active's properties at Green Point and in Bellville, I felt relatively safe to start swimming there again. But at 9.37 am, on 1 September, while I am changing, naked and on my own in the empty change room, here they come again: A_____ and his friend (whose name I still don't know). *Hy lyk goed* (he looks good) they remark brightly to each other as they stroll past me.

I wrote to Virgin Active club management to express my concern. They had assured me that I would be able to use the facilities at Wembley without having to worry about encountering these men. But there they were. What was going on?

A week went by. I received no response at all.

I made some discreet enquiries, relying on friends who knew some of the people on the inside.

The problem, the answer came back, was that Virgin Active management did not know what to do. Their ethics policy did not allow them to disclose the whereabouts of any visiting member without their consent. So they could not respond to my request.

I was not at all surprised. By now I had a pretty solid understanding of how this company negotiated the complex terrain of corporate ethics and moral responsibility.

Eventually I received word that a member of VA's top team was willing to speak to me—off the record. We eventually managed to have a telephone conversation. This person confirmed that I had not been hallucinating: A_____ and his friend had in fact been in my club on the day in question: the one and only time he had ever visited it.

There was not much they could do about it, this person said. Perhaps I could consider going to Constantia, or the club in Tokai instead?

Part 7

Hexagram 29 – "The Abyss"

Aftermath

Slowly the event faded into the past. I had no further encounters with A_____ or any of his associates. Autocorrect eventually unlearned its unhelpful suggestion.

Other aspects of the whole experience proved harder to leave behind. Physical normality returned, but the world as it used to be did not. It was easy, I found, to allow a darkness to settle over things. The adrenalin, the fight or flight response that took over my body in the initial aftershock gave way to something more insidious, more damaging: a dreadful torpor, a queasy malaise. It was not a matter of *giving in* to obsessive thoughts: the obsessive thoughts were there, refusing to relinquish *me*. They were always there, waiting for me when I found myself in a shopping mall parking lot or did my lengths in the pool or drove in the city at night or saw a buff black man, dressed neatly in jeans and a black shirt, walking towards me on the street.

It did not help that I was suddenly aware of the extent to which M_____'s connections had all the time been woven through my entire world. That restaurant where I met Jay after making my statement on the evening of 5 February? A front for his money laundering activities. S____ nightclub, where my stepdaughter liked to hang out with her friends? The same. The private security organisation hired by the Camps Bay improvement district to police the beachfront? Owned by M_____. And so it went. I could mention more details, but some of them still feel too risky to share.

I had entered, I realised, a bleak and horrible world—the world of the reptile brain, for which only two things exist: killing, or being killed. It was if the cold, vicious psychotic energy I first encountered when A_____ leaned across the table and told me *jou fokken poes, ek gaan jou fokken doodmaak* had become part of me, part of my body, as if the man was still sitting there in the centre of my heart: ice cold, malign, immovable; like a tumour. Like a wart.

For a few months I went to a therapist's room in Claremont to participate in something called EMDR. Over and over, she asked me to reimagine key details of the event while following her waving finger with my eyes, switching from right to left and back again. This was how the brain could unlearn trauma, the theory held, by in some way forcing new connections between the right and the left hemispheres of the brain. The sessions helped not at all; indeed, I felt I was retraumatising myself. After doing the 12 sessions allowed by my medical aid, I let it go.

With time, the queasy dark dread I carried with me started to fade a little. Today it is possible for me to visit the shopping centre where I was assaulted without fear.

But it did not leave entirely. It receded to the background, became part of the normal, a little like the twinge that remains in the middle of my back that still prevents me from sleeping comfortably some nights, or like the doubleness in my eye.

I tried, every now and then, to sit down and write; to try to make sense of the whole story, to do what I had always been able to do which was to get a handle on things by *understanding* them, by making them make sense.

But I could not. I wrote and wrote, but whatever answers I tried to find seemed to me trite, superficial, pointless. I was able to get some perspective on the whole matter, and even to find a certain kind of grim humour in it (picture it: here is the feared gangster, known all over town for his savage temper and his cruelty; here is the fuddy-duddy university professor, suddenly getting it into his head to teach this man a lesson in wokeness).

But I could not make it work, partly because I did not trust my own motives. Why was I so invested in writing about this?

Was I seeking vindication, trying to establish my credentials as a Best White, so people would say yes, he is a white male, but he Stood Up Against Racism and paid the price for it? There was something petty and self-serving there that repelled me.

Should I pander to my need to say to the Lindsay Maasdorps of the world, and, yes, to my own colleagues at PLAAS, can't you see I am one of the good guys? To make it all about me, to tell a story in which Vuyokazi was just a prop, a part of my own self-exculpatory narrative?

More to the point, what sense *could* I actually make of the attack? What meaning could I recuperate from it? That shit happens? That South Africa is a violent society and that even white male professors are not safe? That white supremacy works in mysterious ways? I wrote pages and pages of rueful and thoughtful reflections, but they all seemed flaccid to me, prolix and sententious.

One thing was clear to me: I am still white. I am still privileged. I did not regret the stand I took (clumsy as it may have been), but I am under no illusion: I am still as much part of the structures of privilege in this country as ever. I did not regret my actions. But what did that mean? Where did that leave me? I just did not know.

In the end I put the piece away and went on to other things.

Feeling in the dark

SOMETIMES WRITING FLOWS, LIKE TAPPING into a pool of understanding, letting what wants to be said emerge into the world. More often it is a hard and knotty struggle; wresting meaning piece by piece into the open. And sometimes it is like leaning into an icy dark pool, feeling for what is there. Grab it too quickly, and it slips away like a fish between the fingers. You have to wait and let your hand feel the shapes in the dark. And every now and then you bring a stone to the surface: heavy, cold and slimy, and you let it sit in your hand and feel its weight.

Here is one stone: it is not an easy thing to share. It feels like such a small thing. At some point in the last five or six years, I have gradually become aware that I am not sleeping well. I fall asleep easily enough, but after three or four hours I wake, and I wake to dread. It feels as if I have a cold heavy lizard sitting on my heart. My heart pounds, my breath is short, my mind is filled with an odd, untethered, reasonless anxiety, an endless obsessive narrative, joyless and filled with foreboding, as if in the shadow of some dreadful approaching but unspecified cataclysm. Thoughts about work not done, funding not raised, doom approaching. Every night. Every night. Every night.

In the morning it is gone, and I enter the day positively enough. But only for the day: when night comes, I find myself there again, visiting that cold dark lonely moon.

I have learned to deal with it to some extent. I practice a simple form of mindfulness meditation, just being present with my body, with my breath, seeking and eventually finding solace just in the fact of being a body, being alive. *Just be here. Just be here. Just be here.* In time, sleep returns, and by morning I've found my way back to planet Earth.

For a day.

I have not been able to get to the root of it. Sometimes I think it is just the cold light of reality: things in South Africa after all, are not going well at all. Take a look at the world around you: any sane person would suffer sleepless nights! Sometimes I tell myself it's just brain chemicals. Too much cortisol. Age. That could be the case. But there's meds for that kind of thing, and in my experience, while they keep things on an even keel, the trapdoor to the dark still opens every night.

It is only recently, when I found myself revisiting the events surrounding the assault, that I have started wondering if they are connected. Not with the force of sudden revelation, but rather as an intimation, a suspicion, as a spoor to be followed back into the darkness.

Here is another stone: in the years since the events I recount here, the world has changed; or rather, the outlines of what was already there have become more evident. We live now in the time ushered in by Trump, by Modi, by Putin and their ilk. Despite all the talk of neoliberalism you still hear on the left, the fact is that the world order ushered in by Blair and the Clintons and everything they stood for is in tatters. Neoliberal globalisation has been defeated; it has been replaced by something much worse.

One consequence of this change is that we now live much more than we ever did in a world of shadow states and captured governments. The money launderers and the gangsters are stronger than ever. M_____ and his kind are no longer—if indeed they have ever been—confined to the underworld of nightclub extortion rackets in the tawdry corners of Long Street and Somerset Road. Their alliances, we now know, connect them to the very highest echelons of power in this country. When the criminal networks around Jacob Zuma and the Radical Economic Transformation (RET) faction tried to organise a hit on our Public Protector, Thuli Madonsela, the man rumoured to have been approached for the job was none other than the Cape Flats gangster who was A_____'s associate. And though Zuma's faction is (for now) marginalised and Trump is (for now!) out of power, it is clear that they were but a harbinger of what is coming.

Another consequence is that the stable, optimistic political world that I worked in—a world in which it was once possible to believe in rational policy deliberation, in the machinery of technocratic development, in the big and shiny words of development discourse—that world has gone. The disconnect between that world and the superheated, volcanic world of contentious politics has widened and keeps on widening. The gears are still grinding; calls for proposals are still being published, and new buzzwords are being minted every day (building back better! just transition! convivial conservation!). But the crucial bits of reasoning that in development-speak are called the *theories of change*—not theories *about* change but the models that purport to describe how all this research and deliberation is actually going to translate to actual change in the world—these look, in my eyes at least, increasingly implausible and threadbare. The work of policy research and deliberation appears to me more and more a kind of ritual activity; one that brings in the bucks all right, but to what end? Our problem at PLAAS between 2000 and 2015 (that government was ignoring our policy advice) has been replaced by a graver one: what use is winning the policy battles if the basic institutions of government that are meant to implement and drive those policies are in tatters, "captured", dysfunctional and crumbling?

The most popular answer from what remains of the South African left seems to be that if change cannot come from the state ("from above", as folks like to say) it must come "from below"—from "the people" taking power back into their own hands and making change happen through mass organisation.

It is an attractive thought, but try as I might, this simply reads like nostalgia for the good old days of the UDF, when democratic populism was the way to get things done. I am not convinced. For one thing, the conditions that made that kind of mass organisation possible are gone. For another, and rather more pertinently, one particular group of people who happen to be positioned very well to organise and shape any form of popular action from below are those very gangsters. Can one really argue, for instance, as we have done at PLAAS, that the occupation of South African Railways land in Philippi by homeless black shack dwellers represents a nascent form of people's organisation, when it is pretty clearly understood by all involved (but never actually admitted) that the indirect beneficiaries and likely sponsors of that occupation include the taxi drivers' organisations who have no interest in the return to functionality of the commuter train? But that is an inconvenient thought. Much nicer to talk about people's power.

But most of all, all this turning-our-backs-on-the-state, all this romanticism about the need to rebuild the struggle from below seems to be based on blindness to the reality that the biggest crisis we face right now is not simply that the promises of 1994 have not been kept, but that government is collapsing around our ears.

This does not mean that I do not think there is work to be done. There is indeed. But it is the work of repair. It is the work of what the I Ching calls "working on what has been spoiled". Building a society that "belongs to all who live in it" is difficult. It requires forgoing the large gestures and public moral stands of what passes as "radical" thought today. It requires accepting the reality of complicity and being compromised. Over the last few years, I have grown more and more suspicious of the ease with which it has been possible to construct the precarious but still relatively privileged world of tenured academia as the site from which a "radical" critique of capitalism is articulated. I still value the practice of "critique"—the practice of investigating the world in order to help change it—but it seems to me that it can only be of help if it works in a much more complex and modest way, close to the worlds of practice and part of the messiness of the world.

And here is the third and most painful stone, the hardest to acknowledge, which is that I have not been able to take my colleagues at PLAAS along with me on this journey.

This is a complicated matter, and there are many threads to this story. Much is probably due to failures of leadership or skill on my part. But the truth is that the gap that I felt opening up between my colleagues and I on that day in 2015 has only widened. It has become clear to me that the project that informed so much of what we did in the last two decades—challenging the "class character" of agrarian land reform in South Africa—appears to me to have utterly failed. Sure, land and access to land is still a vital issue, but the real need, and the most important flashpoints lie not in the farmlands but in the complex and ambiguous struggles unfolding in our urban areas. Most of all, my own belief—that as writers and researchers working on injustice and inequality in South Africa, we should avoid sweeping ideological critique—that belief has not been shared by my colleagues, or at least not by the most vocal ones.

Or so it seems to me. I have been told that my attempts to raise more complicated, unsettling questions are not needed, are self-indulgent, are just "navel-gazing". (It is not that my views are *wrong*, I have been told, just that they are *unhelpful*, they might alienate prospective partners, or send the wrong message. I am being a "traditional academic", not a "scholar-activist"; my writing is just old-fashioned ivory tower self-indulgence, not part of building the campaigning organisation that we need to be.)

So for now, at least, PLAAS will not enter the morass of compromise, the space between, the ambiguous terrain where the difficult problems are. We will not be *complicit*.

And you know what? It might work. PLAAS is a well-respected organisation with deep networks. Hopefully it will survive these complex times. It may be able to keep going for twenty more years.

It will have to be without me, though.

Part 8

What is at stake

WORDS CAN DO MANY THINGS. They can create connections; they can enforce boundaries. They can heal, and they can hurt. They can bring understanding, or they can occlude, lie, and hide.

So what about these words? What about this essay? Exactly what am I trying to achieve here?

It was easy to find the title: "An Introduction to Violence". That is in part what it is about: my personal encounter, as a privileged white man, with the kind of casual violence that millions of poor black people experience every day in South Africa. Call it a rite of passage. An induction. An onboarding, as they like to say in the business world.

But I wanted a subtitle. In the first draft of this essay, I called it "A tale of fists and words". Clearly this is one of its subject matters. On the one side, words: the hateful and violent words of Vuyokazi's abusers, and also the ways in which I tried to use words to intervene and to make sense, to understand and to engage. On the other hand, fists, because, well, you know why.

But there is much more going on here. As you will by now have seen, the violent encounters around which I have constructed this narrative are not actually my main concern. True: one of my reasons for writing about it at all is to work though them and understand them and (hopefully) to let them go. And also just to be able to say: this happened; it really happened, and I am still here; I survived.

But that is only part of it. Over time I have come to realise that the real importance of what happened is that it is a doorway. A portal.

What I am writing about is an experience of trauma. About societal and personal trauma: one tiny moment in the ongoing violence, structural and physical, that is part of South Africa's reality, and about how it persists. I've already likened it to a tumour sitting in my heart. Or a cancer. It is something that I have allowed to become part of me, that's rooted itself in my being. As I followed those roots, the tangled connections of feeling and association that radiated out from that painful and shocking encounter, I found myself having to ask what had been at stake for me there, what it signified. I realised that, in addition to it being an encounter with the violence that is part of the normal processes of racial oppression in our society, it called me to investigate and think more deeply about who I think I am, and what I am doing.

And so the trail led me back to the little boy on his grandfather's farm, to my encounters with black anger expressed and unexpressed, to my sense, above all, of belonging to a society pierced to the heart with deep divisions: divisions not only of class and of race, of wealth and poverty, but also of remembered pain and embedded violence. Of hurts and angers so deep that it sometimes feels as if they *cannot be spoken*, cannot be understood.

And the trail has led also to the ways in which I have at times felt myself called—perhaps naively, perhaps grandiosely (and sometimes, as you have seen, unskilfully)—to intercede, to step into the space between, to try to hear what has not been spoken, to stand up for civility and respect. To try to be part of the making of a community *that does not yet exist*, but upon which, for me at least, any meaningful way of belonging to this country depends. The story also led me to understand the debt of gratitude I owe to the teachers I encountered on the way; and in particular the black persons—I have named some of them here—who had the grace to address me kindly across the boundaries of ignorance, pain and difference.

Most of all, this process brought to my awareness how much I am invested in the story I like to tell myself about myself—the way I make sense of my decisions and actions, and also how I like to think about what I am trying to do and how I am trying to live. In the ManKind Project, men are encouraged to formulate a "mission of service". Sometimes it feels a bit hokey or awkward, as if one were trying to craft a Mission Statement for a single person rather than a corporation. But it is a valuable exercise in moral clarification and a powerful tool for accountability to self and others. Mine would be something along the lines of: seeking to use the gifts of compassion and understanding to heal a divided world.

As you have seen, the significance of my encounter with those gangsters is all tangled up for me with a broader question about whether and how I can do this work of healing or bridge building at all. I have no doubt that the work of healing, of reconstruction, of transformation, needs to go on. But where do I fit into it? Day to day, in my personal life, I can be part of the process. Small acts of kindness and recognition and all that. But what about *work*? All I can say is that there is at present no agreement between me and my colleagues at PLAAS about how we should be going about it (and whether that is even how we see our role at all).

Also, it is worth thinking more critically about this whole peacemaker thing, all this "understanding the world in order to change it". It is important to recognise that ultimately it is just a story. A role. One way of thinking, among many. One should not cling too tightly to it. Sure, it has its value; it can be an inspiring story. It can also be self-serving, a story that allows me to pass by or occlude my own complicity in the structures of violence. It can be counter-productive, avoiding or bypassing the conflicts that are necessary for resolution to occur. And crucially, it can be self-destructive, part of the endless acting out of a story of victims and persecutors, rescuers and self-sacrificial lambs.

The kyōsaku

UNDERSTANDING, TOO, CAN SERVE MANY purposes. For the Buddhists what they call "Right Understanding" is foundational. Without it, you are in the grip of fantasies, stories and illusions, stuck on the wheel of suffering, doomed to chase after phantoms and rage against fate. But understanding can also serve as an escape, as a defence against unbearable feeling, as a way of putting oneself outside or beyond that which is being experienced.

I have found one useful way of thinking about understanding in the book *Flowers in the Dark*, by a Buddhist nun known as Sister Đẳng Nghiêm. She writes that everyone who has experienced trauma faces the same choice: to try to pick up the pieces of their lives and continue as before, or to stop and turn more intentionally towards healing. Those who take the second choice may find that turning to face pain and suffering can be a way to open into to a greater understanding of life.

Đẳng Nghiêm ("Sister D", as she is affectionately known) is a member of the Order of Interbeing, the school of Buddhist thought and practice based at the Plum Village Monastery in France and founded by her teacher, the Zen monk known as Thích Nhát Hanh. He was a teacher noted for his commitment to social action and engagement with the realities of everyday life, and also for his remarkable personal compassion and gentleness.

There are harsher approaches, of course. In many Japanese schools of Zen a flat wooden stick or slat called the kyōsaku is used to strike meditators who are not sitting upright or who have drifted off to sleep.

A punch to the face may be considered to serve something of the same purpose: as an invitation to be more aware, to wake the fuck up. To be here, now. To be accountable: what are you doing here, and why?

Turning around

So where am I now, and what have I learned?

I have learned a bit more about how violence feels. I know more intimately how shame and rage and powerlessness can linger in your body; how they can become a persistent companion, whispering in your ear, sapping your life and energy.

In a way this is valuable. Though I have long understood *intellectually* the realities of inequality and structural violence in this country, I think I have become more emotionally and spiritually attuned to the personal suffering they entail. So it is a path to compassion, an awareness of what lives outside the bubble of safety I continue to occupy.

I have learned that Sister D is right: that these experiences of violence (structural and physical, "slow" and explosive, of words and of deeds) are not things that can be left behind. That if I try to do that, all that happens is that I let the trauma work in the darkness, like Ged's shadow in that first *Earthsea* book, lurking in the corners and whispering words of doubt and self-betrayal in my ear.

And I have been complicit in this. I have at times allowed myself to betray myself. I have shut my mouth. While I may sometimes have spoken up for others, I have many times not stood up for myself. I have at times even doubted whether I, as a "white" man, have the right to speak at all.

Hence this essay. As young Ged learned, running away from the shadow does not work: all that happens is that you burn out, give away your power. The only way forward is to stop. To turn around. Not to conquer the shadow, but to meet it, to embrace it; to, as the Plum Villagers say, "take care" of it.

And I have learned that it can be done. Sister D knows a thing or two. The practice of mindfulness, her teacher used to say, is comprised of two things: stopping, and deep looking. Both are difficult. But they are also very simple. All it takes is patience, and diligence, and learning step by step to recognise, accept and transform, through kindness, forgiveness and compassion, the mental habits that perpetuate pain.

I have also learned that there is no such thing as individual trauma. Sure, some of the events I described here impacted on me painfully. But they are merely a small manifestation in my own life of the patterns of cruelty and violence that are still reverberating in our society, 30 years after the transition to democracy, 112 years after the Land Act, 191 years after the abolition of slavery, 336 years after the arrival of the Du Toits on these long-peopled shores.

Those social reverberations, too, are not going to go away. They are all around us: the memory of violence suffered and perpetrated, living on in bodies and in minds. They will not leave of their own accord. Neither can they be banished by some transcendent act of redemption or reconciliation. They are our inheritance.

We have a simple choice. We can choose to try to ignore and deny them. We can choose cynicism or political and social despair, endlessly recreating the future in the image of the past.

Or we can choose the work of repair.

Hexagram 18: "Working on what has been spoiled"

Acknowledgements

Stephen Bloch, Colleen Crawford Cousins, Thomas Cousins, Jay Douwes, André du Toit, Marijke du Toit, Zimitri Erasmus, Barnor Hesse, Shakti Malan, Julia Martin, and Kaushik Sunder Rajan.

Works cited

Adams, Douglas. *The Hitchhiker's Guide to the Galaxy.* 1st edition, Del Rey, 1995.

Davis, Rebecca. *Best White and Other Anxious Delusions.* Pan MacMillan, 2015.

Golden, Lisa. "If You Are A White South African, Please Read This". *The Daily Vox*, 23 Feb. 2016.

Laclau, Ernesto, and Chantal Mouffe. *Hegemony and Socialist Strategy: Towards a radical democratic politics.* Verso, 2001.

Le Guin, Ursula K. *A Wizard of Earthsea.* Illustrated edition, Clarion Books, 2012.

Nghiêm, Sr Đăng. *Flowers in the Dark: Reclaiming your power to heal from trauma with mindfulness.* Parallax Press, 2021.

Piketty, Thomas. *Capital in the Twenty-First Century.* Translated by Arthur Goldhammer, 1st edition, Belknap Press, 2014.

Louw, NP van Wyk. *Versamelde Gedigte.* 1st edition, Tafelberg/Human & Rousseau, 1981.

Varoufakis, Y. *Adults in the Room: My battle with the European and American deep establishment.* Vintage, 2018.

Ware, Vron. *Beyond the Pale: White women, racism, and history.* Verso, 1992.

Wilhelm, Richard. *I Ching Or Book Of Changes.* Translated by Cary F Baynes, Penguin Books, 1989.

White, TH. *The Once and Future King.* 8th printing edition, Berkley Books, 1968.

Andries du Toit is a researcher, teacher and writer based at the School of Government at the University of the Western Cape. Over the last thirty years he has done extensive research and writing about poverty and inequality in rural South Africa. He lives in Kalk Bay.

Author photograph by Julian Goldswain

www.ingramcontent.com/pod-product-compliance
Lightning Source LLC
Chambersburg PA
CBHW070310230426
43664CB00015B/2708